Daniel Grant

Home Politics, or the Growth of Trade

Considered in its Relation to Labour, Pauperism and Emigration

Daniel Grant

Home Politics, or the Growth of Trade
Considered in its Relation to Labour, Pauperism and Emigration

ISBN/EAN: 9783337133016

Printed in Europe, USA, Canada, Australia, Japan

Cover: Foto ©Suzi / pixelio.de

More available books at **www.hansebooks.com**

HOME POLITICS,

OR THE

GROWTH OF TRADE

CONSIDERED IN ITS RELATION TO

LABOUR, PAUPERISM & EMIGRATION.

BY
DANIEL GRANT.

LONDON:
LONGMANS, GREEN, READER AND DYER,
PATERNOSTER ROW.
1870.

ENTERED AT STATIONERS' HALL.

PREFACE.

This book has been written with the desire to keep it entirely removed from party politics. The great problem—How are the people to find work and food—is a distinctly social one, and is so important for all classes of society that any effort which can be made to solve it is worth the labour. I had no pre-conceived theory to uphold, and throughout I have stated the facts simply as I found them; the deductions I have ventured to draw seemed to flow naturally, but how far the conclusions are accurate I must leave others to judge.

Daniel Grant.

March, 1870.
   12, Cleveland Gardens,
      Hyde Park.

CONTENTS.

The Condition of the People - - -	1
Free Trade and Reciprocity - - -	10
The Growth of Trade - - - - -	19
Our Future Trade - - - - -	62
Population and Food - - - - -	78
Labour - - - - - - - -	93
Pauperism - - - - - - -	106
Emigration - - - - - - -	126
India - - - - - - - -	146
Résumé - - - - - - - -	168

HOME POLITICS

OR THE

GROWTH OF TRADE.

CONDITION OF THE PEOPLE.

AMONG the many great questions that are now pressing for solution, there is one that imperatively demands an answer: How are the people of our country to be fed? How are the people to obtain both work and food? Under all phases and through all kinds of circumstances this question is ever presenting itself—it appears in those thrilling episodes of human misery, when the tortured and the broken, the half-starved and the reckless, hopeless of the future, flinging on one side all questions:—seek refuge in death: it appears in that sense of sullen but half muttered defiance, which is more or less distinctly traceable amongst a large mass of our population; it appears in the outbreak of the Famine Fever, the continuous increase of our pauper returns and an ever growing taxation. The reason why this question should take precedence of all others, is to be found in the broad fact that it goes to the root of the happiness or the misery, the well being or the destitution of the great mass of the nation.

However much we may disguise or slur over the fact, we have to stand face to face with difficulties, probably as profound as those which swept over this land, previously to the repeal of the Corn Laws. It is well whilst there is yet time, that we should grasp the problem in its entirety and do our best to find the solution. The question travels over a very large surface of ground. It asks what has been the cause of the past growth of our trade; and why has it now ceased to expand? It asks what is our probable future with regard to the commerce of the world? and which way does our path lie through the dangers that menace us?

It forces these questions on us, not as abstract problems on which themes may be written and theories discussed, but as the great practical necessities of life which are as essential to our existence as the air we breathe. It has been asked before, and it may be asked again: is it possible that there are in this very London of ours the elements of revolution? Who shall answer? But, whether it be so or not, there is no question that hunger makes strange havoc with pet theories, and men, who are placable and kind, when they are passingly comfortable, are dangerous and deadly, when they crave in vain both work and food. It cannot be the wish of the great landed interests of this country, that the large questions connected with territorial property and their right of holding, should be bandied about from mouth to mouth, when men are maddened by the sense of want. It cannot be either their wish or interest that the fierce sense of wrong, implied in the fact of class legislation, should be driven home to fester amid sorrow and despair. The names that many of them bear, who by labours at the bar, or services in the battle field, are traditional elements of intellect and courage; and there is no higher testimony to the aristocracy of our land than to say, that, representing as they do the relics of the middle ages in laws that are at once hard, grasping and unjust, they have contrived by their broad common sense, large courtesy and far reaching fairness, to stand amongst us to-day as a class greatly honored; but if the sense of sorrow and misery that now overshadows our land should deepen, as most probably it will; if the cry for aid;—aid by thought; aid by care; aid by law; should arise and be not responded to, the monitions and warnings that are everywhere around us will have spoken in vain, and history will chronicle the results.

Let us for a moment think what are the conditions of our poor to-day. Apart from the question of our agricultural population, whose almost hopeless lot is best told by the simple fact, that in many places the luxury of meat is comparatively unknown; apart from the questions of special emergency, such as the cotton famine, or the East End Emigration Society, which has been brought into existence for the purpose of relieving the great mass of destitution and poverty in that neighbourhood; apart from all such special and exceptional cases, we have the general sense of depression and want everywhere spread around us. It is not necessary to dwell on the scenes of human misery, where wholesale suicides or cruel murders, mark the profound despair or those who lay trembling on the confines of want. It is equally unnecessary to recall those verdicts that appear time after time at coroner's inquests under the simple but expressive phraseology—"Death from Starvation." It is not necessary to recall these things, because the newspaper press of the country drives these truths home without stint and without compromise; but it may be important to remember that the individual cases, which thus come to the surface, are known only by accident, and that the great mass of misery that suffers and dies,—dies and tells no tale. Occasionally and by accident the curtain is drawn on one side, and we see into the midst of the life of poverty that surrounds us; and we then know by the glance thus afforded us what the general life must be: wasted by poverty, decimated by fever, shattered by want; and it thus rises before us, in the full force of its appeal to that sense of human sympathy which is common to us all.

But the general acceptance of the positions here stated will be aided by a few facts. Let us see what the barometer of pauperism has to tell us. Our pauper population in

   1866 was - 920,344
   1867 „ - 958,824
   1868 „ - 1,034,823

and the number is still increasing; yet these numbers shew that our pauper population has increased by 114,479 persons in two years or at the rate of more than 1,000 per week. Even this large increase does not indicate the exact extent of poverty,—it points to the still wider field of misery that exists among the classes from which pauperism is fed. Let any one think what is the state of destitution through which a man passes, before he is willing to accept relief and allow himself to be branded as a pauper. Those who know the working classes best, know the profound abhorence they entertain of the Workhouse. Any privation, any sorrow, any destitution rather than that; and the natural inference is, that the pressure of want is not only severe but has been long enough sustained, to have swept away all articles of clothing, as well as all household goods, before the sufferers bend to their fate. Let us take some few instances of what the present condition shows. As one illustration of the state of destitution take the following:

"*Monday, March* 8, 1869.—At the last meeting of "the Chester Guardians, Mr. Brittain, one of the relieving "officers, stated it as his belief that there never was "so much destitution in the city, even in an inclement "season, as there was at the present time. He knew "poor people who were living on Indian meal and a 'little buttermilk.'"

The same general illustrations is afforded by this extract taken from the *Pall Mall Gazette* of September 30, 1869 :—

"Dr. Mitchell, reporting to the commissioners in Lunacy "for Scotland, states that on the occasion of his visit to "Shetland, he saw much stronger and deeper signs of "poverty than he had ever seen before. In the parish of "Unst the year's poor rate is no less than 7s. 1d. per pound "of the gross rental. When the taxes, charges and burdens "on land are added to this, he was assured that less than "one-third of the rental will be left the proprietor. All over "Shetland the poor rate has been rapidly and steadily "increasing during the last twenty years—the increase in "some parishes being 700 or 800 per cent. In the parish of "Lerwick, it is said to have risen since 1845 from £40 to "£900. After his visit to the county he wrote to the "chairman of one of the parochial boards, urging the "extension of relief to a melancholic who clearly needed "care and treatment in an asylum. His request received "prompt attention, but the chairman, a gentleman most "charitably inclined, said, 'in our dealings with the poor we "have always to consider our own impending ruin.'"

The same journal in referring to the general state of pauperism has the following.—

"*July* 14, 1869.—Our great industrial centres are "apparently applying with a free hand some dangerous "palliative of distress, the money doles of the relieving "officer, unwarned by the bitter experience of the agricultural "counties of the southern half of England. Wait awhile, "and Lancashire, at her present rate of pauper development "may range with Wilts, Dorset, or Devon."

The following is extracted from the *Lancet* of October 9,

1869 : and adds one more illustration of the general destitution incident to the Metropolis:—

"FAMINE FEVER.—The interesting communication of "Dr. Murchison, which we print in another column, draws "attention to the renewed prevalence in London of a "disease which, fortunately, has of late years been rarely "seen in this country. Relapsing fever may be broadly "said to be the product of destitution pure and simple; "but once established, it becomes communicable by con- "tagion. As regards the spread of the disease in London, "the statistics of the Fever Hospital undoubtedly point, as "Dr. Murchison observes, to the fact that the disease is "becoming distinctly epidemic,—the numbers of admission "for the months of May, June, July, August, and September "being 4, 3, 7, 15, and 34, respectively; and 7 admissions "having taken place on October 1st. The poorer classes of "London are, we fear, threatened with a terrible scourge "during the approaching winter; for not merely is there "great danger of relapsing fever taking formidable dimen- "sions, but, as Dr. Murchison reminds us, such an event "is nearly always accompanied by an increased diffusion "of typhus."

In addition to all these, the reports from every part of England indicate a great and growing pressure, not only on the absolutely poor, but on the trading classes immediately above them. In one parish of London, that of Lambeth, it has been found necessary at one sitting to issue 400 warrants of distress, in order to obtain payment of the poor rates. At another place, that of Willesden, a magistrate stated that he had done nothing all one day but sign summonses and warrants for the same purpose. Facts of this kind are not open to statistical accurracy, but they are almost beyond the necessity of statistics, for they are matters of universal acceptance, and can be more or less distinctly verified by us all.

The general recognition of our present condition of pauperism and labour is best illustrated by the great number of pamphlets that issue from the press and by the acknowledged utterances of our leading men; although the reasons and explanations given by them are strangely at variance. One gentleman finds the cause of our present distress to be drunkenness; another finds it in the want of education; a third in the present condition of the land; a fourth in Trade Union combinations; Mr. Bright thinks it is connected with the want of cheap cotton, whilst Lord Overstone thinks it is an ordinary check and that it will right itself. In the face of such divergencies, with a stagnant or retrograde trade, and with a large mass of our population unemployed, it seems time that we should collect our facts and see what they teach us.

The possible results of a condition, akin to our present, is thus referred to in Mr. John Stuart Mill's *Political Economy*, when speaking on the question of Wages, there is the following:—

"If the growth of the towns and of the capital "there employed, by which the factory operatives are "maintained at their present average rate of wages "notwithstanding their rapid increase, did not also absorb "a great part of the annual addition to the rural popu-"lation, there seems no reason in the present habits of the "people why they should not fall into as miserable a "condition as the Irish previous to 1846; and if the "market of our manufactures should, I do not say fall "off, but even cease to expand at the rapid rate of the "last fifty years, there is no certainty that this fate may "not be reserved for us."

In the first place, it is undeniable that we have a pauper population considerably in excess of one million of people; in the second place, it is unquestioned and unquestionable, that our export trade has not grown for more than three years :—

> Our exports in 1866 were £188,917,536
> „   1867 „   181,183,971
> „   1868 „   179,463,644

But, to understand the force of these figures, it must be clearly remembered, that England cannot feed her own people;—that we have been under the necessity of importing foreign corn since 1793, and that the probability is, that one-half of the entire population of our country is fed by corn, grown on foreign soil. This corn that thus feeds our people, has to be paid for by some means; and it is paid for by the means of our export trade. So long as our export trade continues to grow at a sufficiently rapid rate, all goes well; but, so soon as that trade ceases to grow, the pressure of an ever increasing population trenches on the means of life, and pauperism and destitution increase.

The significance of the position will be best appreciated by the recognition, that our clear nett gain, as a mere matter of population, is about 220,000 per annum, or at the rate of more than 4,000 per week, the statistics being:—

> 1865 - - - - 20,990,946
> 1866 - - - - 21,210,020
> 1867 - - - - 21,429,509
> 1868 - - - - 21,649,377

showing a clear increase of 658,431 since 1865. The question, therefore, before us, is not only how are we to feed our existing population, but how are we to feed one that is continuously increasing and increasing at the rate here indicated. Our trade during twenty years, 1847—1866 had answered all questions, because it had grown with a rapidity sufficiently great to find work for the ever increasing population; but, as its growth for the time seems definitely checked we stand face to face with the problem: how are the people to find at once both work and food?

The results that will follow from our present position are very evident, for, as population continues to grow, whether there is work or not, it will be obvious that we may look forward to a continual increase of pauperism and destitution until some counteracting agency comes into play. The question will then arise, in what do these counteracting agencies consist? To obtain an answer, it will be necessary to weigh the question of Free Trade and Reciprocity to trace out clearly the causes of the growth of trade, specifying those which are under our own control and those that will, in the ordinary course of events, continue to develope trade by their own action. Beyond these, it will be necessary to trace out the present condition of labour in our own country; the relation of population to food; the probabilities that surround the question of foreign competition as affecting our future trade; the question of emigration and colonization, as affording the proper means of removing a certain portion of our surplus population and at the same time developing trade ; and lastly, the value of our Indian dependency. But all these points will fail of carrying their necessary weight, unless the conviction is unwaveringly fixed, that the time has come when the country requires definite and vigorous efforts to restore it to its own place amongst the growing powers of the world, and that, in order to achieve this result, it is necessary to see our exact position.

The first point which will be discussed is Free Trade and Reciprocity.

CHAPTER I.

FREE TRADE.

THERE is no term more misused than that of Free Trade. From many platforms, in many newspapers and from the mouths of many men, who are accepted as the leading exponents of far reaching political thought, the term Free Trade is used with a laxity and carlessness that cannot be too strongly condemned. No fact is more patent than the one that, either from ignorance or indifference, men are applying to Free Trade arguments and reasonings which were never enunciated by its founder, and which are not legitimate deductions from its principles. Free Trade, in its broadest and fullest sense, means the absolute freedom for every country to deal with every other country, without the intervention of either import or export duties. It asserts still further that such a course of commercial policy is distinctly beneficial to all concerned; but it neither asserts nor does it imply, that the reduction of import duties in one country will be the cause of the growth of the export trade of that same country, except so far as that reduction will stimulate reflex action.

It seems almost idle to point out, that the reduction of an import duty upon any one article of home consumption—such as sugar for instance—can have no reference as to the growth of any one of our exports—such as iron for instance—except so far as the mere incidental relationship of the countries whence the sugar comes, may be stimulated by the purchase of more iron goods arising from the increased profits of an increased trade. The reduction of an export duty is based on the assumption, that the cheapness and freedom, induced by the removal of the duty, will stimulate increased consumption; but such duties are almost non-existent, and for all practical purposes may be left unnoticed. The reduction of an import duty finds at once its justification and explanation, by the growth of the imports on which the duty has been reduced. If the import duties on tea had been reduced and the consumption of tea had not increased it would have proved that, with the classes who drink tea, the duty did not prejudice the sale, and as such, the reduction of duty would have been a mistake, as it would have wasted a given amount of revenue. But when we find, as we do find, that when the duties are reduced upon the great necessaries of life, the rebound is large and vigorous, no further justification is required as to the wisdom of the abolition of the duty. The broad fact, that each reduction of our import duties has been followed by increased consumption, in some cases to so large an extent as to enable the reduced duty to produce a larger revenue than it did under the higher rates, establishes once and finally the wisdom of such legislation. It is necessary to insist that this is the justification of the reduction of our import duties; because there is a grave tendency to appeal to the growth of our export trade as a justification of the reduction of our import duties. The two points are broadly and essentially distinct. Our export trade grows by, and is dependant upon, a series of special causes which is altogether distinct from the question of the reduction of our import duties. In what these consist is attempted to be shewn in the next chapter.

All duties are in themselves evils, but which must exist, and solely, for the purposes of revenue; being justifiable, only on the ground, that they afford the most certain and the least onerous mode of collecting such revenue. By a mere accident, some duties on manufactured goods have acted as a protection to home manufactures; and by an entire transition of thought, the duty, instead of being viewed as a means for producing revenue, has come to be viewed as a means for protecting home manufacturers from foreign competition. It is therefore wise, for all who accept the doctrine of Free Trade, to admit that the reduction of a duty may be distinctly prejudicial to a special class who have been fostered by the existence of the duty into a state of dependance. The reduction of the duty on silk is said to have produced a large amount of misery at Coventry and Macclesfield and men clamour for its re-imposition; by a curious coincidence, numerous meetings have been held in France to effect the same purpose in that country. In each country the special injury, inseparable from change of tariff, has produced a clamour, which marks a sense of depression and want, but which is absolutely worthless as a matter of argument. And it may be very justly asserted that the outcry of the silk-weavers of our country is, in one sense, a direct justification of the removal of the duty; for it proves conclusively that our own manufacturers were unable to compete on fair terms with France, and therefore the whole of the country was indirectly taxed to uphold the special branch of trade carried on by the silk-weavers.

The same general feeling, that has been expressed in connection with the Cobden Treaty, was expressed by the agriculturists at the time of the projected repeal of the Corn Laws: it was asserted throughout the whole of the agricultural districts, that the farmers could not hold their own if the import duties on corn were removed. The Corn Laws were, however, repealed in spite of the clamour of the agriculturists, and what has been the result? Our agriculturists have not only been enabled to hold their own, but have improved their position year by year ever since, and the farmer of to-day is not only much richer but, as a class, the whole character is changed: from being slow, careless and heavy, he has become shrewd, scientific and active. The nobler qualities, that often lie latent in the English nature, have been developed by necessity, and the man who, according to his own idea, was unequal to the task of fighting the battle of competition without aid, has proved himself more than equal to the emergency. The same results will follow with reference to silk weaving, when the consequences of change have had time to right themselves. When the circumstances settle down to their natural level, the men, who are to-day desponding, will look around and find, that, as the field is perfectly open, they will be able to hold their own by using the energy, care and taste that are inherent in us as a people. Already some facts clearly show, that they are beginning to see such a way out of their difficulty. And it is quite clear, that as we buy our silk free of import duty (the French can be no better placed) and therefore any protective duty would be simply a premium on incompetence;—a condition, which is not only unsound, but one, that our own manufacturers would be the very first to repudiate, when brought clearly home to their minds. The difference between the French and ourselves is simply a difference of machinery and skill.

It is of course quite conceivable, that very harsh results are at times to be traced to the rapid removal of an import duty on manufactured goods. Many men who have been reared in a trade, and who know no other, find, when old age is creeping on them, that their trade is passing from them by an Act of Parliament. It would seem that, placed as our country at present is, some action should be taken to soften the severity of such legislative changes. It may be necessary, as a matter of broad policy, to remove a special duty; but it can never be wise to produce misery in so doing.

There are some countries in which Free Trade has had some opportunity of realizing the ideas of those who uphold its doctrines—in Europe notably in the Hanse Towns and Holland—and it has proved itself true to the principles of its originator. These states have reduced the duties on their imports and, as a consequence, their imports have grown.

It appears necessary to insist again and again upon Free Trade axioms, as there is a distinct tendency to uphold changes on grounds that will not bear analysis. It has been more or less definitely asserted, that the growth of our export trade has been due to our recent legislative enactments, meaning by that, that our reduction of import duties has been the cause of the growth of our export trade, the result is, that, when our trade ceases to grow with its accustomed energy, men turn round and attack Free Trade for the shortcomings, for which Free Trade is in no sense responsible. The term "Free Trade" first obtained its currency during the agitation for the repeal of the Corn Laws, the point aimed at being Free Trade in Corn; but when that result was achieved, the men who had aided in the passing of the great measure had become known as Free Traders and thence has originated the very open phrase of Free Trade. The wonderful growth of our export trade since 1848 had dazzled men's eyes so completely, that they neither asked nor cared to know how it came about. They assumed, with a grave respectability, that it was due to Free Trade; what was implied by the term, what were the limitations, or what was the general reasoning on which it was based, few cared to inquire and still fewer cared to say. Circumstances have now somewhat changed. For the first time during the last twenty years our commerce has ceased to expand and it is everywhere asked—Why is this? How comes it that the powers that have fostered our trade, until it has become the envy of the world, have ceased to operate? At a late Free Trade meeting at Manchester Mr. Wilson, in quoting statistics to show the value of our Free Trade policy or what passes current under that name, gave, with admirable clearness and force, the statistics illustrative of the general growth of our trade; and, so far as the reasoning had reference to the advantages derived by the great mass of the people from the abolition of duties on all the necessaries of life, the position was absolutely unanswerable; but when from the same figures deductions were made, as illustrative of the cause of the enormous growth of our export trade, the result aimed at was neither so conclusive nor so satisfactory, and the reason why is not far to seek. So long as the question rested upon the removal of import duties and the growth of our imports, the figures were clear and the connection positive and satisfactory. One tabulated form after another answered one question after another, until the brain wearied of the endless iteration. Beyond this, there was the great moral truth, that the toiling millions of our country have the unchallangeable right to buy food in the cheapest markets of the world. But when the orator, growing with his subject, spread out before his enthusiastic audience the growth of our export trade—marvellous in its very fecundity—and claiming to be the direct result of Free Trade action, the reasoning halted. With an instinctive sagacity, men asked, and asked justly, what is the connection between the reduction of import duties and the growth of export trade? Where is the link? What is the sense of dependance that unites the one to the other? To say, as men have said, that the growth of our imports is the direct stimulus to the growth of our exports, is to say that which the veriest tyro in the knowledge of statistical facts will know to be inaccurate. A reference to the Board of Trade returns will show what such assertions are worth. The totals of our imports and of our exports bear some relationship to each other, but the imports from, and the exports to, individual countries vary to an enormous extent. But it is said, if the growth of our trade be not dependent upon the connection between our imports and exports, on what does it depend? How comes it, that more or less coincident with the repeal of our various import duties, there has ever been an increase in our export trade? The answer is, firstly, that this is not strictly accurate; and secondly, that a series of other causes was at play whose influences are distinctly traceable. With regard to the first, from 1840 to 1848, a period of nine years, the total growth of our export trade was as follows:—

1848	-	-	-	-	£52,840,445
1840	-	-	-	-	51,406,430

Being a nominal increase of - £1,434,015

And yet, during these years, our Free Trade policy had been more or less definitely at work—the duties on corn, rice, coffee, timber, currants, wool, glass, sugar, cotton, butter, cheese, &c., had either been repealed or largely reduced. If the reduction of our import duties be a cause of the growth of our export trade, how came it that no more definate evidence of it was shown during the nine years here specified?

To all this there seems but one answer, that is, that, either from the apparent insignificance of the subject or from the pleasure derived in following out the wondrous harmony that always belongs to a great general principle, the bulk of those, who have been instrumental in bringing our country to a due recognition of the acknowledged value of Free Trade, did not think it worth while to trace out the more common-place causes that absolutely underlie the development of all trade. But, as different times are now dawning upon us, and, as the claim for reciprocity is loudly proclaimed, it becomes necessary to trace out more definitely some of the causes that have developed our trade, in order that we may clearly understand on what influence we can rely for its further growth.

Throughout the whole of the discussion it has been assumed that Free Trade really exists; yet nothing can be further from the fact. Free Trade exists in part in England, but as regards both Europe and America it has substantially no existence. With certain exceptions heavy import duties are still levied on English goods throughout the continent generally. The same remarks apply with reference to America, so that our position is this: we, as a country, buy in the cheapest markets, and the great bulk of the nations of the Continent and America do not. The government has just issued a return of the duties levied on English manufactures, entering foreign ports, and which embraces the following countries: Russia, Sweden, Norway, Denmark, Zollverein, Hamburg, Bremen, Holland, Belgium, France, Portugal, Spain, Italy, Papal States, Austria, Switzerland, Greece, Turkey, United States. With one exception, that of Hamburg, every article of English manufacture has to pay duty. In one case as high as £56 10s. 4d. per cwt., and on a large number of cases at 15, 20, 25, 30, and 40 per cent. *ad val*: so that the check upon the growth of our manufactures is both very strong and very marked. There is one point, on which those who claim reciprocity, are distinctly right. They see, and seeing claim, that other nations should trust us as we trust them; but the error of this position is, that we have no power to compel other nations to follow out our doctrines and any attempt to punish them by reimposing import duties would simply recoil on ourselves. If import duties were imposed as a mere matter of reprisal, the actual result would be that all consumers throughout the country would be taxed for the mere support of a particular trade. Besides which the mere fact of a tariff being imposed as a coercion would in itself be a mistake, for though something may be gained by judgment and tact, but little can be hoped for from threats and anger. The position of our manufacturing industry is one of grave difficulty, but we shall achieve more by calm sense and good temper, than we shall ever approximate to by quarrelling.

There is no doubt that if the foreign tariffs could be reduced the immediate effect would be a large increase of our export trade. But, as that is one of those things still lying in the future, we can only recognise that Free Trade has not done its work, and that, as we cannot compel other nations to modify their tariffs against their will, our business is to leave these points to the action of the future, and to trace out other causes that will stand us in equally good stead. And as a preliminary, it will be necessary to analyze carefully the various conditions connected with our past growth of trade, for which purpose we will pass to the next chapter.

CHAPTER II.

THE GROWTH OF TRADE.

It has been asserted that the evidence already deducible from our export trade points to the existence of a series of special causes influencing and developing its growth. The question now before us is to understand clearly in what they consist, and how and under what circumstances they have come into play. In order that the point may be distinctly understood, it will be wise for us to take some special year from which all comparisons shall be made; for that purpose the year 1840 has been selected, it being previous to the development of Free Trade doctrines; and, as the comparison will be carried on up to the present year, 1869, we shall have before us the whole range of figures and events on which our present commercial policy is founded.

To obtain a clear conception of a subject, it may be necessary, at times, to analyse it carefully into its component parts. In applying this course to the question before us, we find that our exports from 1840 to 1868 show a growth of about 128 millions: our exports in 1840 being £51,406,430, and our exports in 1868 being £179,463,644. The questions then arise,—how have our exports grown; to what countries have they gone; and what special causes can we trace by which their growth has been accelerated or retarded. As a broad statement of the case, the increase of our exports has been mainly in those sent to France, Holland, Hanse Towns, Russia, Turkey, Egypt, Japan, California, the United States, Australia, India and China; and the growth in the exports to these respective countries is more or less directly coincident with certain special causes that came into play at the time their trade was developed. For instance, the growth of our trade with France was distinctly due to the Crimean War and the Cobden Treaty; that with the Hanse Towns to our Exhibition and their own reduced tariffs; that with Russia and Turkey, to the Crimean War and to the relationship established with those countries by the influence of our government and capital; that with Japan and Hong Kong to the opening of free ports; that with Australia and California to the gold discoveries; and that with India and China to the military operations connected with our position. The statistics of our trade with each of these countries will be taken separately in detail, and traced through to their legitimate results. By this means we shall arrive at a sound conclusion on the principles that more immediately affect the growth of trade.

It will be well, as a preliminary step, to have before our minds the one broad fact, that the producer and consumer form the basis of all trade; and that the merchant, wholesale dealer, exporter, agent, and retail seller are simply middle men by whom, for the sake of convenience, the goods pass from the producer to the consumer. We have also to shift our mind away from the totals of exports, which are only the chronicled results—to the consideration of the causes that produce sale amongst the consumers themselves. When we say that so many hundreds of millions of yards of cotton have been exported, we have to bring our mind to watch in detail, how the great mass becomes disintegrated piece by piece until we notice where a few yards are sold by the retail seller to the poor consumer. That point forms the turning point of commerce. The causes that influence the development of such sales are the causes that influence our whole export trade; for the commerce of the world is based on the necessities of the many, not on the fancies of the few; and whatever cause can be pointed out as naturally acting on the great body of the people may be accepted as a cause that developes our bulk trade.

What, then, are the causes that directly affect the development of trade amongst consumers? 1st, Knowledge of the existence of manufactures; 2nd, knowledge of the people by whom these are produced; and, 3rd, the opportunity to purchase. With regard to the first, it does not matter how good, how cheap, or how useful any goods may be, if they are not known to those to whom they are fitted, no trade takes place. Nor does it matter how superb an article may be, unless it fulfils the conditions of sufficient publicity the same result will follow. If a man had a statue by Phidias or a picture by Michael Angelo and placed it in a back street, it might remain for hundreds of years unsold and unknown; but if the same statue or picture were placed in a leading thoroughfare of London or Paris, it would soon find a purchaser: because the knowledge of its existence would be sure to reach those who desired to possess it. A nation is in a back street whose intercourse with other nations is limited, and whose means of communication are imperfect. And any cause, such as railways, that tends to remove these impediments is a cause that developes trade.

It adds but little to the force of this assertion to say that, it is an accepted axiom, that a tradesman requires to make his wares known, in order to bring their use, beauty or fitness, clearly and definitely before those whom he wishes to become purchasers; and should he fail or be prevented doing this, his trade will stand still. If, on the contrary, he takes the opposite course, and bring his wares well under the notice of other men, he will create a want and supply it at the same time. How many of us are there who go on from year to year without some given article, until by accident we see it in a shop window, are struck by its appropriateness and purchase it, and ever after it becomes to us a necessity.

Such a case is a simple illustration of the processes by which trade grows; and the public recognition of this principle, which bears evidence, in our export returns, of having aided the growth of our past export trade, first found its utterance in our International Exhibitions, which are nothing more than great national bazaars.

The illustrations given are simply the illustrations of the influence the goods themselves have upon the development of trade by being brought into sufficient notice. Such a cause is perfectly apart from any question as to who the producer or seller may be; but, beyond the mere influence of the goods themselves, there is always the secondary influence mutually exercised by peoples. So long as a nation suffers from prejudice and the want of knowledge, so long as one people stands to another in the relationship that they neither know nor care to know, so long does trade languish. Any cause that removes these obstacles, developes trade: and no cause has more clearly produced these results than War.

It will be readily admitted, that the knowledge that one nation has of another will vary very largely under the action of different causes. For instance, it will be quite clear that the sort of knowledge the Turks, as a people, had of us as a people, would be very different after, to what it was before, the outbreak of the Crimean war. The mere contact of the two peoples, under such circumstances, would inevitably create a sympathy different from that which previously existed. The same remarks will apply to Egypt, France and Russia and, with some modifications, also to India and China, and the results are manifested in our trading with these various countries. It has been asserted that war has a distinct influence on the Growth of Trade. The statistical proofs of this fact will appear further on, detailed in connection with the various countries that have been selected; but the broad question is, how comes it, that war should produce such results? The answer is, war acts through a series of causes. Not only are people brought distinctly into contact with one another;—not only are conditions established which underlie all commercial life; but the power of a country to buy or sell, the characteristics that belong to her, her capacities of growth, her undeveloped resources are all more or less brought vividly into view, and thus stimulate trade. Notably has this been the case with Turkey—and the result has been, that Capital, the great sinew alike of war and peace, has flowed continuously into her coffers. Loan has followed loan and each successive advance has tended to bind our commercial relations more closely and to lift her, so far as she can be lifted, into a position of respectability and power. The mere fact, that the strong brains of English Capitalists are thrown into the question, is in itself an element of growth, and an element that probably would not have existed but for the outbreak of the Crimean war.

Let us take another case; the one the most opposed to the probability of the view here enunciated;—that of Russia. Previous to the outbreak of war, Russia had stood to this country as a great menace; the power wielded by the Czar had been developed with such untiring energy and skill, that the subtle diplomacy of the Muscovite was a favourite illustration amongst all European diplomatists. This reputation for power and ability was aided by the anomalous position at that time maintained alike by Prussia and Austria. Their complicity in the dismemberment of Poland bound them by a tie, none the less real, because it was equally dishonorable. But connected as the German powers were, at that time with Russia, by treaties, intermarriages and blood relationships, it seemed almost a possibility that the words of the 1st Napoleon might be realized—that Europe would become either Cossack or Republican:—and taken in conjunction with the events of 1848, and the utter and unsparing stamping out of the very embers of the Revolution, it seemed more probable to be the former than the latter. The results of the Crimean war changed all this. The power of Russia was shattered and the morale of her position destroyed. A change was produced in her people both extensive and distinct, and the position in which we stood after the war was marked by the general rising of our status as a nation—not only throughout Europe—but perceptily throughout Russia herself; and thus the stand point of our commercial interests had risen, from the mere fact that we had conquered.

Beyond the immediate action of war in the development of trade, there is that more silent and more subtle influence which belong to the civilising agencies that we, as a nation, are exercising upon all other nations with whom we come in contact. Without arrogating to ourselves any special supremacy, there can be little doubt that at the present time all things English have a certain repute and fashion. To what an enormous extent this and similar influences affect our export trade is not at first sight clearly apparent. But let us take two or three instances and see whither they lead us. At the present moment, throughout the whole of Europe, as well as in India and America, English thoughts and English habits are largely gaining ground. In Germany our language is being taught in the great majority of the schools; in France the present Emperor has stamped English idiosyncrasies on French thought, even to the bull terrier and jockey club. At our universities the same influence is at work, and we find there the heirs presumptive to various thrones mingling in English life and imbibing tastes that will inevitably be stamped in some degree on the people whom they are intended to govern. All these causes combine and recombine towards one end,—that of creating a demand for English productions.

It may and probably will be urged that this growth of trade is due to the goodness of our manufactures. In one sense this is true. Our manufactures would not be permanently sold if they were not good; but if they were ever so good, from the point of view which is now being urged, they would not obtain the same sale if they were not fashionable. The term fashionable is here used in a very open sense—meaning, not the mere follies that are prevalent to-day and thrown aside on the morrow; but that largely appreciative sense that has a tendency to infuse itself into the very life of a people, and which is only imbibed by them when time has established the warranty of its goodness and soundness. We may also refer here to the influence of the English travelling public. Whatever else they may do, they carry our language, our habits, and our manners throughout Europe, and by their own wants, as well as their general influence, aid the cause here indicated. The result is to be traced in the great silent growth of our trade over the whole of Europe, as illustrated by the rise of our exports through the Hanse Towns and elsewhere.

We now pass to the consideration of the influence that the Gold Discoveries and Emigration have had upon our Export trade. The result of the Gold Discoveries in California and Australia were, at the time, most marked, so far as the power exercised on the minds of all intending emigrants. The public mind was influenced to an extent rarely seen, and men of all classes and conditions of life threw up steady pursuits to follow the dream of a probable Eldorado. The results show themselves in the returns. In 1851, the year of the discovery of gold in Australia, the number of emigrants who left England for Australia and New Zealand were 21,532.

1852 - - - - 87,881
1853 - - - - 61,401
1854 - - - - 83,237

The mere fact that this mass of population was poured into a new country would naturally produce an increased growth of our exports. And the results are apparent in the amounts themselves. Our exports to Australia in

1852 were - - 4,222,205
1853 - - - 14,513,700
1854 - - - 11,931,352

And the same general facts appear with regard to California. In

1846 our Emigrants - 82,239
1847 - - - - 142,154
1848 - - - - 188,233

And our exports during the same years were as under:—

1846 - - - 6,830,460
1847 - - - 10,974,161
1848 - - - 9,564,909

The reason why the statistics to Australia are taken for one year later than for America, is that the great distance between Australia and England throws the returns so many months later than would be the case with America. The connection between our own country and America being so rapid and intimate, the action of any cause at once manifests itself. With regard to California, there is some difficulty in getting at the permanent influence the discovery of gold exercised either upon emigration or our export trade, as the returns are so made up as to blend California with the United States. It also happened that the discovery of gold in California was coincident with the great mass emigration from Ireland, which immediately followed the Irish famine in 1845—1846. We have therefore two difficulties before us. The one, the imperfection of the returns; the other, the coincidence of another cause of emigration. But, as the assumed value of the discovery of gold in any particular part of the world is based on the ground that the direct influence of such discovery is to develope trade through the instrumentality of a large emigration to that particular place, any cause which happens to act simultaneously to produce the same result, may be classed with it; as the principle point, that the discovery of gold enables us to clear up, is the direct and tangible influence exerted upon our export trade through the aid of a large emigration.

With regard to the influence of emigration, it will be quite clear, that those, who have been nurtured in our habits of life, who have our tastes, manners, and customs, will carry their predilections for our special manufactures into any new home they may found. The thoughts and feelings that are moulded into our being through the plastic life of childhood and ingrained into us through the more enduring, if less sensitive, time of our manhood, will remain with us, as an inalienable portion of our being through all circumstances and in any part of the world. No education is stronger than the education of habit; it is with us a second life, to be worn out only by slow decay; and this quality links our emigrants to us, and in so doing aids our manufacturers. The artisan, who lands at New York or Melbourne with little money and no friends, whatever else may have failed him, has fully tested the trustworthiness of his clothes and his tools; and with the instinctive reverence that ever clings to the known and tried, he will greet with pleasure in a new world and amid new faces the familiar names of English manufacturers. In one sense we are all conservatives; we hold to that which we have tested and not found wanting, and that great mass wave of population that flows ever from our shores, to be absorbed by other lands, still clings to us by this feeling of the past. The conditions here asserted are mere matters of reasoning. What are the facts? Let us take the two cases now chosen, that of Australia and that of the United States and California, and place in opposite columns the growth of our exports and the mass of our emigration, year by year, so that we may have the circumstances clearly before us.

The first thing that shows itself, in looking over these returns, is the absolutely stationary character of our export trade with Australia from 1840 to 1849, the returns in those two years being almost identical in amount. The next point is, that the trade showed distinct signs of retrograding up to the year 1847, and that during that time the emigration and exports fell off together. It is also apparent, that when emigration again set towards Australia, our exports again rose; and they sprang into full force and power under the influence of the gold discovery in 1851. The rise of our exports in the two following years to more than five times their previous amount will be a clear illustration of the influence of that discovery. In 1853—4 the exports from England to Australia had been largely in excess of the demands, and the consequence was that in 1855 our exports receded, until the natural impulse of growth again forced them upwards. It would be tedious to point out all the minute influences that go towards making up the sum total of an export trade; and also the various causes that affect it, such as good or bad harvests, agreement or disagreement between the houses of Legislature; and yet all these tend to elevate or depress returns. Enough will have been done if the statistics show clearly the connection between emigration and export trade; and also the special influence exercised on that trade by the discovery of gold. The next case—that of California—is less simple in its results, but it illustrates more vividly the immediate action of such discoveries.

AUSTRALIA.

Year.		Emigration.	Exports.
1840	- - -	15,850	£2,051,625
1841	- - -	32,625	1,336,626
1842	- - -	8,534	958,952
1843	- - -	3,478	1,307,062
1844	- - -	2,229	791,994
1845	- - -	830	1,244,121
1846	- - -	2,347	1,441,640
1847	- Irish famine -	4,949	1,644,170
1848	- - -	23,904	1,463,931
1849	- - -	32,191	2,080,364
1850	- - -	16,037	2,602,253
1851	Discovery of Gold	21,532	2,807,356
1852	- - -	87,881	4,222,205
1853	- - -	61,401	14,513,700
1854	- - -	83,237	11,931,352
1855	- - -	52,309	6,278,966
1856	- - -	44,584	9,912,575
1857	- - -	61,248	11,632,524
1858	- - -	39,295	10,463,032
1859	- - -	31,013	11,229,448
1860	- - -	24,302	9,707,261
1861	- - -	23,738	10,292,771
1862	- Exhibition -	41,843	11,944,506
1863	- - -	53,054	12,498,534
1864	- - -	40,942	11,857,213
1865	- - -	37,283	13,339,241
1866	- - -	24,097	13,643,326
1867	Dead Lock at Melbourne	14,466	9,613,739
1868	- - -	12,809	12,071,435

The same general remarks that were made with reference to Australia will apply also to the returns of the United States and California. Emigration and exports are clearly and distinctly co-related. The first great impulse in our exports occur in 1847, the year of the discovery of gold in California and the commencement of that great mass of emigration that set for seven years so steadily from this country towards the United States. It must be understood that emigration is only considered as one cause—and a cause that will be modified one way or the other, according as any second influence is in favour of, or opposed to, the development of our trade. For instance, the outbreak of the Civil War in 1861 and the closing of all trade with the Southern States, manifested itself by reducing our exports one-half. In this case the Civil War acted by destroying our existing trade with the Southern States; and so has reduced the apparent influence of our emigration. The converse holds good in 1866, when, under the influence of speculative capital brought into play through the general mania of the time, our exports reached their highest point. What is intended to be asserted is, that our export trade is due to a series of causes, of which emigration is one; and that these causes combine and recombine to produce a total result. That, in order to trace those causes out clearly, it is necessary to take them one by one and watch their influences under circumstances when they are the least disturbed. For that purpose Australia and the United States have been chosen under the aspect now delineated, as illustrations of the influence of emigration, combined with the discovery of gold.

It is curious to note how the tide of emigration ebbs and flows. Under the impulse of the panic induced by the famine of 1845, it rose to its height in the years 1850, 1851, 1852, and 1853, and then gradually receded, until, in 1858, it reached its former level; it has again bounded forward, and promises in the next year or two to reach its highest point.

UNITED STATES AND CALIFORNIA.

Year.		Emigration.		Export.
1840	- - -	40,642	- - -	£5,283,020
1841	- - -	45,017	- - -	7,098,642
1842	- - -	63,852	- - -	3,528,807
1843	- - -	28,335	- - -	5,013,514
1844	- - -	43,660	- - -	7,938,079
1845	- - -	58,538	- - -	7,142,839
1846	Irish Famine	82,239	- - -	6,830,460
1847	Discovery of Gold in California	142,154	- - -	10,974,161
1848	- - -	188,233	- - -	9,564,909
1849	- - -	219,450	- - -	11,971,028
1850	- - -	223,078	- - -	14,891,961
1851	Exhibition	267,357	- - -	14,362,976
1852	- - -	244,261	- - -	16,567,737
1853	- - -	230,885	- - -	23,658,427
1854	- - -	193,065	- - -	21,410,369
1855	- - -	103,414	- - -	17,318,086
1856	- - -	111,837	- - -	21,918,105
1857	Financial crisis in England	126,905	- - -	18,985,939
1858	- - -	59,716	- - -	14,491,448
1859	- - -	70,303	- - -	22,553,405
1860	- - -	87,500	- - -	21,667,065
1861	Outbreak of Civil War	49,764	- - -	9,064,504
1862	- - -	58,706	- - -	14,327,870
1863	- - -	146,813	- - -	15,344,392
1864	Limited Liability Act.	147,042	- - -	16,708,505
1865	- - -	147,258	- - -	21,227,956
1866	- - -	161,000	- - -	28,499,514
1867	- - -	159,275	- - -	21,826,703
1868	- - -	155,532	- - -	24,410,184

Let us now pass to the considerations of the influences that Exhibitions are supposed to have exercised on trade. At the opening of the Exhibition of 1851, the whole of the circumstances, that could produce a successful result, were brought freely into play. Imperial pageantry, international courtesy and diplomatic suavity were all made to aid in the development of a royal idea, and the success of the Exhibition, simply as an Exhibition, was unequalled. Not only as a mere show was the effort successful; its influence on trade was also very large. For the first time in history, nations were invited from all parts of the world to take part in rendering homage to mere commercial pursuits; and for the first time it was proclaimed as a principle, that trade was paramount. Dreams of universal peace and universal brotherhood were largely indulged in, until they were disturbed by the rude utterances of war.

Yet with all this, there were some results that were left unchallenged. The Exhibition ennobled commerce: men from various parts of the world had learned to look upon trade, and more particularly English trade, from a point of view they had never previously approached, and the result was that trading relations were not only cemented but extended. The ideas associated with our Palace of Industry were those of royalty, wealth and elegance, and all these were aided by the very structure of the building, as it rose in its fragile beauty spanning the noble trees and looking out to the clear sky beyond. To ourselves as well as to others it was a great lesson, the influence of which has not yet died out. It taught us not only what we could, but what we could not do, and it placed before us by illustrations, stronger than any language, how much inferior our art productions were to those of our compeers: and from that teaching has emanated our South Kensington Museum and our present demand for Technical Education.

All these things influence trade, both directly and indirectly. In an earlier part of this chapter it was pointed out, that the personal knowledge of buyer and seller forms an important link in the growth of trade, and in one sense the first Exhibition aided this. Men, who for years had known each other by name, came to know each other as a matter of fact, and thus built up relations that produced a mutual good. The mere prestige of the "world's bazaar" brought men from every quarter of the habitable world and they carried away with them to their distant homes the memory of English productions, that bore fruit then and has borne fruit since. At the time, amongst the whole of our manufacturers it was recognised as an unchallengeable fact, that the Exhibition had stimulated trade, that orders were plentiful and that its success was great.

The statistics do more than bear this point out, the bound in our exports is both clear and decisive. It will be necessary to notice here that the direct results of the Exhibition would not be manifest until the year after it closed, and would most probably extend twelve months beyond. The Exhibition did not close until the end of the year, the orders given during the time would be delivered partly in the year 1851 and partly in 1852 and the return orders some months later, so that the effects would appear in the following years. The statistics here given show very markedly the growth of our exports at the particular epochs.

    Our Exports in 1851 were £74,448,722
          1852 ,, 78,076,854
          1853 ,, 98,933,781
  Showing an advance in the two years of £24,485,050

The same results are apparent in the two years after our second Exhibition:

Our Exports in 1862 were £123,992,264
      1863   „   146,602,342
      1864   „   160,449,053

Showing an advance in the two years of £36,456,789

In looking at these figures it must be remembered, that the results here manifested embrace the action of other causes besides that of the Exhibition. For instance, in 1851 the furore of the gold fever in Australia was in full force, and there was also flowing from our shores the great emigration that followed the Irish Famine; both these causes would combine to swell the returns of 1852, 1853. At the second Exhibition another influence was at work, the results of which are quite as manifest, viz.: the operations brought into play in connection with Limited Liability. This act came into operation in November 1863, was immediately taken up by speculators and was in full force in 1864. The result is manifested in the returns of our export trade in that year, and also in those of 1865, 1866. To some it may appear dubious that the Limited Liability Act should have this influence; a little examination will shew the reason why. There is no question that, at the time of the speculation mania, companies for every conceivable purpose were floated into existence, some useful, some stupid and some mere frauds; but, whether good, bad or indifferent; whether they paid dividends or not; whether they ruined shareholders or not, during the time of their existence they stimulated trade. To what extent they acted may be gathered from a statement that appeared in the Money Article of *The Times*, in which it was stated that during the continuance of the mania, companies, representing a capital of 800 millions, had either been projected or actually brought out. A mere moiety of the amount here named would be sufficient to explain a large increase in speculative trading.

The companies that were brought into being ranged

from those that were absurd by their triviality to those that propounded to their shareholders the idea of constructing railways and rebuilding cities. All were equally available for the mere purposes of creating a direction and robbing the credulous. Amongst those who dealt in such operations it was considered of great value to give a look of mercantile reality to the transaction; and for furthering such views foreign contracts, foreign railways and foreign banks were made to float largely on the surface; and, as a rule, they had some connection, more or less real, with our foreign trade. If a railway were projected, it would be necessary to make some show of work; and the consequence was that rails, carriages, engines, tenders, &c., &c., would be bought from our manufacturers, and would figure in the total of our export trade. The same remarks can be applied to a series of cases, and would furnish an explanation of some portion of that large growth of our export trade during the time referred to.

Let us now pass to detailed causes; the general reasoning that connects war and trade has already been given. We have now to trace out the results, and see how far it has actually operated in the growth of our exports. The various wars, that fall within the time specified, 1840—1869, are the Crimean War, the China War and the Indian Mutiny. The New Zealand War, the Abysinian War and the Caffir War are omitted, because the reasoning which will be true of the larger, will be true of the smaller, and also because, as a substantial result affecting our export trade, we can afford to disregard the latter.

Let us take a case which will include the largest variety; and place most conspicuously the results of the action of war within our grasp. For that purpose the Crimean War has been selected; it was the most important as well as the longest sustained, and its influence on France, Italy,

Turkey and Russia herself can be clearly traced; the facts in each case bearing out the inference now sought to be deduced.

FRANCE.

The country which has been first taken is that of France, for the reason that it embraces three points: the first is the action of war, which affects the exports, from 1854 to 1857; the second is the influence of the Cobden Treaty, which affects our exports from 1860 to the present time; and the third is the influence of our speculative mania of 1864, 1865, and 1866. In each case, it will be found on examination, that our exports rose very clearly and distinctly in connection with each of these three causes.

It will be seen in looking over the figures that our exports show little or no variation from 1840 to 1853, with one exception, that of the year 1848, at which date they receded to one-half their usual amount. The explanation is to be found in the fact that the year 1848 was the year of the outbreak of the Revolution, and, as a consequence, great slackness of trade and a profound sense of insecurity were general throughout France. When the first burst of its influence had passed away, trade once more resumed its usual conditions, and our exports stand at the ordinary amount, and at this standard they remained until 1853. The year 1854 saw the outbreak of the Crimean War, and our association with France in the struggle was at once manifested in our returns, which immediately rose about half a million; the next year our exports were doubled, and at this height they remained until the close of the war. The great impulse to trade connected with our struggle gradually faded out, until our exports had receded to what might be considered their normal amount, an amount less than that which was reached during the height of the war, but still considerably

FRANCE.

Year	Event	Value
1840		£2,378,149
1841		2,902,002
1842		3,193,939
1843		2,534,898
1844		2,656,259
1845		2,791,238
1846		2,715,963
1847		2,554,283
1848	Revolution	1,024,521
1849		1,951,269
1850		2,401,956
1851	First Exhibition	2,028,463
1852		2,731,286
1853		2,636,330
1854		3,175,290
1855	Russian War	6,012,658
1856		6,432,650
1857		6,213,358
1858		4,863,131
1859		4,754,354
1860	Cobden Treaty	5,249,980
1861		8,895,588
1862	Second Exhibition	9,209,367
1863		8,673,309
1864	Limited Liability	8,187,361
1865		9,062,095
1866		11,700,140
1867		12,121,010
1868		10,633,721

in advance of what it had been previously to the outbreak of the war itself. The final results would appear to be, that war developes new relations which continue to act, although with diminished force, after the original cause is entirely removed. The next cause that influenced our exports with France was that of the Cobden Treaty. It came into operation in 1860, and under its influence our exports in two years made an advance of nearly four millions; and although the full amount has not been permanently maintained, yet the result is sufficiently clear to indicate the influence that treaty has exercised upon our commerce with France. The action of our Limited Liability Act and the general speculative mania manifested itself in our exports to France, as well as to other countries.

It is difficult, on looking at the points here indicated and contrasting the time they came into play with the actual returns of our exports, not to feel that they are related as cause and effect. It seems equally impossible, on the theory of the general cause of Free Trade, to make any sensible explanation of the phenomena that present themselves to our notice. Our trade with France remained stationary for 14 years and yet, during the whole of that time, Free Trade had been more or less definitely in action; our exports then doubled themselves. We naturally ask what is the cause? We do not suppose that orders drop from the skies, or that some fairy has created an imaginary want; men of common sense believe, and believe very naturally, that there is a cause for every change, even where a tangible explanation is not forthcoming; but when the known requirements of war are considered and our capacity as a manufacturing country to satisfy those very requirements, the rise of our exports through the action of war seems inevitable and, as a matter of fact, the orders given to this country by France for all war materials were very large.

There is one point here that ought to be borne in mind in order that the results may be put down at their proper value. A cause of any kind may be in operation some months before its effects are visible, and the results will continue, after the cause has ceased to act. Let us illustrate this. Orders for goods whenever given, if representing any large amount, will usually take some months to deliver, and they will only appear in our exports when shipped from this country. In the present instance a portion of the goods that appear in any year's returns, say 1855, must have been ordered in 1854, so that an allowance of time must be made before the actual results appear in our export returns. The same remarks will apply with reference to the continuance of a cause even after its apparent action has ceased; let us push the same point further. Suppose that our manufacturers had contracted with the French government for given quantities of supplies—those contracts must have been made on the footing that the war would have to be fought out, and as its duration, until actually settled, must have remained an uncertainty, all contracts would be made on full war conditions; and the moment the war ceased, the orders then existing would take some number of months before they were completed. The result would therefore be, that the influence would not at first sight be so apparent, and would remain an influence after the cause, that brought it into play, had entirely ceased to operate. This actually coincides with the facts, our exports show no great expansion in the year of the outbreak of the war, but they appear in force for 12 or 15 months after its cessation. The actual influence of war on our export trade will be most apparent when we bear in mind, that for 14 years our trade with France had not grown at all, and that the year after the outbreak of the war, our exports with France had more than doubled themselves.

TURKEY.

Our trade with Turkey evidences the influence of two causes: the first, that of the Crimean War; the second, that of our last Exhibition. With reference to the first, our exports to Turkey do not show any growth from 1840 to 1854, the years 1844, '45, '47, '48, '49, '50, all figure in our exports for larger amounts than the years immediately preceding the outbreak of the war. So that, taking the fourteen years here referred to, 1840—1853, we may assume that, the differences which appear are differences arising from the ordinary fluctuations of trade, and not those that indicate the increase or decrease arising from fresh influences. It is worth noticing that war was almost identical in its action on France and Turkey. In both cases there was a moderate increase in our export trade in the year of the outbreak of the Crimean War; but in the year following there was a remarkable expansion. In the case of Turkey the cessation of the war produced the immediate effect of a falling off in our exports; but in the case of France the same result was not manifested for some time after, being due to the fact that the prominent position of France necessitated larger and more permanent arrangements, which, as a consequence, required a longer period before they were fully completed. On the outbreak of the war our exports to Turkey rose three-quarters of a million; the next year they doubled themselves; and although they receded from that amount, they never again sunk to their original level. When they reached their lowest point, the effects of the Exhibition of 1862 began to be felt, and our exports again rose and have since permanently maintained their position.

TURKEY.

Year	Value
1840	£1,164,386
1841	1,254,945
1842	1,489,826
1843	1,729,777
1844	2,319,605
1845	2,246,855
1846	1,749,125
1847	2,363,442
1848	2,664,281
1849	2,373,669
1850	2,515,821
1851	1,937,011
1852	2,079,913
1853	2,029,305
1854 — Outbreak of Crimean War	2,758,605
1855	5,639,898
1856	4,416,029
1857	3,107,401
1858	4,255,612
1859	3,750,996
1860	4,408,910
1861	2,987,800
1862 — Exhibition Year	3,487,761
1863	5,714,550
1864	5,977,918
1865	5,677,830
1866	6,346,041
1867	5,482,153
1868	6,293,782

Up to the year 1845 the returns of Turkey include Greece, Moldavia, and Wallachia.

ITALY.

The statistics of the Kingdom of Italy have not been detailed out, as they are so blended with those of Austria and the Papal States that they cannot be easily distinguished; but, those, who are curious on the matter, will find, on reference to the returns, the same general principle manifesting itself as appears in the returns of France and Turkey.

RUSSIA.

It may be here noticed that the actual exports in 1840 are about £400,000 more than they were in 1853; but as the actual return of exports from year to year varies from minute and often very trivial causes, it is deemed unnecessary to take any notice whatever of any amount either above or below an average, if it can be fairly assumed to be a mere fluctuation, not a definite increase or decrease.

From 1845 to 1854, not only had there been no increase, but the whole appearance of our exports indicated a steady falling off. The years when our exports reached their highest were 1844 and 1845, and from those years the exports show a gradual decrease, indicating either stagnation or retrogression, until the actual outbreak of the Crimean war. With regard to the effect of war on Russia, the result will speak for itself. Immediately on the peace our exports assumed a higher point than they had held for some years previously to the war, and then advanced with great rapidity for the three following years. The force of the impetus that the war had given to our trade then sank slowly away, until the year of the Exhibition, 1862, when our exports again rose, and since then have advanced without ceasing.

RUSSIA.

Year		Amount
1840		£1,602,742
1841		1,607,175
1842		1,885,953
1843		1,895,519
1844		2,128,926
1845		2,153,491
1846		1,725,148
1847		1,844,543
1848		1,925,226
1849		1,566,175
1850		1,454,771
1851		1,289,704
1852		1,099,917
1853		1,228,404
1854	Outbreak of War	54,301
1855	War	
1856	Peace	1,595,237
1857		3,098,819
1858		3,092,499
1859		4,038,696
1860		3,268,479
1861		3,041,448
1862	Exhibition	2,070,918
1863		2,695,276
1864		2,846,409
1865		2,923,006
1866		3,176,656
1867		3,944,035
1868		4,250,721

EGYPT.

The position that Egypt occupies is essentially different from that of Turkey, and is one of those cases where a series of causes combines to produce a total result. There seems to be little difference of opinion as to the fact that the Viceroy of Egypt has exhibited and still exhibits great energy and considerable ability in his government. He has also manifested a clear perception of the value of an intimate alliance with England and France; and the result is everywhere apparent in the general internal organisation of his kingdom, as well as in his active endeavours to develope its trade. In this attempt he has been aided by the planning and carrying out of our overland route to India. The mere fact, that Egypt forms the highway between ourselves and our dependency, with its 135 millions of people, is a tangible reason why our exports to that country should grow. Egyptian commerce has also been largely aided by another influence—that of the outbreak of the Civil War in America. For many years Egypt, like Brazil, had furnished our markets with a moderate quantity of cotton; but the entire cessation of all supplies from the Southern States, consequent on the war, forced our manufacturers to look to other countries for that staple of which they were thus suddenly deprived. Egypt answered to the call, and furnished us with considerably increased quantities, whilst, at the same time, the value of the cotton itself rose with great rapidity, as the figures subjoined will show:—

	Cotton.—Value per cwt.
1860	£3 15 6
1861	4 4 9
1862	7 1 4
1863	10 11 8
1864	12 15 3
1865	8 16 1
1866	8 14 3

This increase of wealth, the natural result of our existing commercial arrangements, aided the development of our export trade.

EGYPT.

1840			£79,063
1841			238,486
1842			221,003
1843			246,565
1844			402,101
1845			291,850
1846			495,674
1847			538,308
1848			509,876
1849			638,411
1850			648,801
1851			968,729
1852			955,701
1853			787,111
1854		Outbreak of War	1,253,353
1855			1,454,371
1856			1,587,682
1857			1,899,289
1858			1,985,829
1859			2,175,651
1860			2,479,737
1861			2,278,848
1862		Exhibition	2,405,982
1863			4,406,295
1864			6,051,680
1865			5,990,943
1866			7,556,185
1867			8,198,111
1868			6,068,569

CHINA.

There have been two Chinese wars, the one in 1840 the other in 1860. The influence of the first war was supplemented by the opening of the port of Hong Kong, and was manifested in the fact, that our exports within two years reached the highest point they ever attained before the outbreak of the Indian Mutiny. The second great impulse on our trade with China occurs in 1859, the year when England and France were preparing their joint expedition; and this rise in our imports is to be accounted for by the fact that goods were shipped from England for the purposes of, or in connection with, the war itself, which took place in the middle of the next year (1860). After the war was over the same result followed as was apparent in our trade with France after the Crimean War; our exports sank slowly; not to the level they had occupied previously to the outbreak of the war, but lower than they had been during the time the actual influence of war was at work. From that point they have since rebounded and have grown continuously to the present time.

This expansion coincides with the time when the influence of our second Exhibition came into play, and affords one more illustration how causes blend one with the other. The assumption, that our Exhibitions have influenced our past trade, appears warranted, not only by the general thought that underlies all such gatherings, but by the mode in which our exports to particular countries have risen at these periods. It is worthy also to note that the influence of our first Exhibition manifested itself on the countries near home, whilst our second Exhibition acted upon those that were scattered throughout the more distant parts of the world, such as China, Japan, Brazil, &c.

It may be said, that the growth of our trade with China is due to the reduction of our duties on tea. It may be wise

CHINA.

Year	Event	Amount
1840	Outbreak of War	£524,198
1841		862,570
1842	Opening of Port of Hong Kong	969,381
1843		1,456,180
1844		2,305,617
1845		2,394,827
1846		1,791,439
1847		1,503,969
1848		1,445,959
1849		1,537,109
1850		1,574,145
1851		2,161,268
1852		2,503,599
1853		1,749,597
1854		1,000,716
1855		1,277,944
1856		2,216,123
1857	Indian Mutiny	2,449,982
1858		2,876,417
1859		4,457,373
1860	Second China War	5,318,636
1861		4,848,657
1862	Exhibition	3,137,342
1863		3,889,927
1864		4,711,478
1865		5,152,293
1866		7,477,091
1867		7,468,278
1868		8,498,966

These returns include our exports to Hong Kong.

that this view of the case should be briefly inquired into. It is curious, but none the less true, that the immediate effect of our reduced duties, was not to create an immediately increased demand. Our imports of tea are as follows, and the date of reduced duties is marked with an asterisk :—

1853	lbs. 70,735,135
*1854	85,792,032
1855	83,259,257
1856	86,200,414
1857	64,493,989
*1858	75,432,535
1859	75,077,451
1860	88,946,532
1861	96,577,383
1862	114,787,361
1863	136,806,321
*1864	124,359,243
1865	121,271,219
*1866	139,610,044
1867	128,026,807

It will be noticed, that in each case the year following the reduction of the duties on tea, the imports are lower. Any probable or reasonable explanation is difficult to give, excepting that the demand for tea is largely dependent upon influences broadly removed from the mere question of the reduction of duty. The consumption of tea, as of all other necessaries of life, is dependent upon two causes: first, the gross increase of our population, and, second, the general condition of the people. The causes that affect the condition of the great mass of the people, will affect the totals of our imports of the necessaries of life. When trade is very prosperous, and when, as a consequence, population increases rapidly, our imports will rise in proportion, being stimulated by the action of prosperity. When men are in full work and at good wages, the question of extra duty on a pound of tea does not produce any marked influence to stop its sale; but when poverty and distress fall upon them, when pauperism rises rapidly, such influences affect the whole mode of living, and definitely arrests the consumption of the necessaries of life. Viewed from this point, the variations in our figures explain themselves; looked at as a whole, the imports of tea show a steady advance, the fluctuations up and down being probably due to mercantile speculations and the variation of quantities held in bond. It would therefore appear, from a review of all these circumstances, that the advance in our exports to China must be considered as being dependent upon causes altogether apart from the question of imposition or removal of the duties upon the special produce of that country.

The considerations that have now been advanced tend to show how the influence of war has acted upon the development of our export trade to the various countries whose returns have been subjected to examination. It will be well before finally closing this portion of the question, to recognise that the consideration of the action of any cause, such as war, is accepted, by the great teachers of Political Economy, as being judged quite apart from its moral bearings.

No man of ordinary feeling will do otherwise than deprecate the existence of a state of war. Devastation, misery and rapine have and ever will follow in its train. But the consideration of the secondary causes that flow from, though not contemplated by war, is a question that appears at once legitimate and wise. What reason can there be why we should hesitate to follow out the action of those secondary causes, whose silent but beneficial influence tends to further the progress of that great civilizer—Trade? In such a sense, and in such a sense only, has war been viewed in the relationship it bears to our commerce. In life all causes are more or less distinctly co-related, the operation of to-day ramifies through a thousand channels, and produces consequences on the distant future that were never intended; thus, from despotism has sprung freedom, and in the blood of our martyrs have been written the articles of our faith. When viewed in this sense, the consequences that flow from the action of war may be accepted without shrinking, and may be regarded as being in harmony with the great teachings of the past, which show us how the wars of Imperial Rome laid the foundations for the civilization of the world.

This digression seemed necessary to prevent misconception of the sense in which war was viewed. We will now return to our last illustration, that of

INDIA.

Following the same course that has been adopted with regard to the returns of other countries, we find that the outbreak of the Mutiny produced an immediate effect upon our exports;—they rose the same year more than one million. In the next year they advanced more than five millions. This increase was, on an average, maintained until the Exhibition of 1862, when our exports again rose another five millions; and that amount has been substantially maintained from that time to the present. From 1840 to the outbreak of the Mutiny, a period of seventeen years, our exports had advanced about $4\frac{1}{2}$ millions. Since that date, a period of twelve years, our exports show a permanent advance of more than ten millions, and this advance remains in full force, in the face of the gigantic failures incidental to, and connected with, the Bank of Bombay.

INDIA.

Year	Event	Amount
1840		£6,023,192
1841		5,595,000
1842		5,169,888
1843		6,404,519
1844		7,695,666
1845		6,073,778
1846		6,434,456
1847		5,470,105
1848		5,077,247
1849		6,803,274
1850		8,022,665
1851		7,806,596
1852		7,352,907
1853		7,324,147
1854	Russian War	9,127,556
1855		9,449,154
1856		10,546,190
1857	Indian Mutiny	11,666,714
1858		16,782,386
1859		19,844,920
1860		16,965,292
1861		16,411,756
1862	Exhibition	14,617,673
1863		20,002,241
1864		19,951,637
1865		18,260,413
1866		20,009,490
1867		21,805,127
1868		21,211,343

HANSE TOWNS.

Hamburg and Bremen are the *entrepôts* of Europe, and the returns that appear under this heading must be regarded as representing a portion of the general trade that is distributed throughout the whole of the Continent. Reference has before been made to the growth in the appreciation of English manufactures, induced partly by our status as a nation, partly by the goods themselves and partly by association. The influence of these causes, blended into one, would manifest itself in the increased trade through those ports which may be accepted as partially representing the centres of distribution for all Europe. By a coincidence the tariff of the Hanse Towns was reduced in the year of our first Exhibition, so that this cause must be joined to the others. We must also note and make allowance for one other influence, which is continuously on the increase, viz., the development of the railway system throughout Europe.

It has justly been said that steam is the great civilizer, and the railway system the great revolutionizer, of the world. Not only are barriers broken down, time economized, and countries linked together that were previously widely separated, but the teaching that springs from such causes is ever present. It brings before men, in phases that cannot be blotted out, the constant growth of thought and the constant stir of enterprise, and, despite the difference of names, makes Europe one great whole. The energy and force, inseparable from all railway life, must tend to quicken the latent activities of the people. It will be at once obvious, that the mere increase of facilities must exercise a large influence on the various countries, by bringing them into more perfect union, and thus enabling commerce to be more rapidly carried on. The action of these causes, when combined, afford a sufficient explanation of the development of our trade through the Hanse Towns.

HANSE TOWNS.

Year		Value
1840		£5,408,499
1841		5,654,033
1842		6,202,700
1843	These returns include Hanover	6,168.038
1844		6,151,528
1845		6,517,796
1846		6,326,210
1847		6,007,366
1848		4,669,259
1849		5,386,246
1850		6,755,545
1851	Exhibition	6,920,078
1852		6,872,753
1853		7,093,314
1854		7,413,715
1855		8,350,228
1856		10,134,813
1857		9,595,962
1858		9,031,877
1859		9,178,399
1860		10,364,237
1861		9,298,463
1862	Exhibition	9,740,336
1863		10,806,092
1864	Limited Liability	13,418,826
1865		15,116,658
1866		13,555,988
1867		17,229,251
1868		19,320,647

HOLLAND.

"In the case of the Dutch Tariff, the liberal system was introduced in 1850. Further reductions were made in the years 1854 and 1862." Our trading with Holland had shown no development from 1840 to 1851; over the whole of these years we have slight fluctuations, but nothing more. The years 1841, 1842, 1843, and 1846 all show larger amounts of exports than the remainder of the years, including that of 1851. We may therefore fairly assume that the trade with Holland was absolutely stationary, until the new influences of the Exhibition and the reduction of its own tariff came into play. It seems only fair to consider these two causes as acting in unison. For instance, the reform of the Dutch Tariff took place in 1850, yet the next year shows no advance; the returns for the two years being almost identical in amount, whilst the two years that follow the Exhibition show an advance of nearly one million. The truth seems to be, that these two causes form the real explanation.

Attention has more than once been drawn to the growth of our export trade in connection with the Limited Liability Act, and illustrations of its influence through the years 1864, 1865, and 1866, appear in the returns of Holland, France, Egypt, Hanse Towns, Belgium, and United States, and can also be traced, although less definitely, through a large proportion of our dependencies. The influence of the speculative mania, incidental to the years referred to, made itself felt, not only in company gambling, but through the more direct avenues of legitimate trading: in the one case dying out with the mania that brought it into existence, and, in the other case, founding new channels of commerce that have still retained their force.

HOLLAND.

Year							Value
1840	-	-	-	-	-	-	£3,416,190
1841	-	-	-	-	-	-	3,610,877
1842	-	-	-	-	-	-	3,573,362
1843	-	-	-	-	-	-	3,564,720
1844	-	-	-	-	-	-	3,131,970
1845	-	-	-	-	-	-	3,439,035
1846	-	-	-	-	-	-	3,576,469
1847	-	-	-	-	-	-	3,017,423
1848	-	-	-	-	-	-	2,823,258
1849	-	-	-	-	-	-	3,499,937
1850	-	-	-	-	-	-	3,542,632
1851	-	-	Exhibition	-	-	-	3,542,673
1852	-	-	-	-	-	-	4,109,976
1853	-	-	-	-	-	-	4,452,955
1854	-	-	-	-	-	-	4,573,034
1855	-	-	-	-	-	-	4,558,210
1856	-	-	-	-	-	-	5,728,253
1857	-	-	-	-	-	-	6,384,394
1858	-	-	-	-	-	-	5,473,312
1859	-	-	-	-	-	-	5,375,468
1860	-	-	-	-	-	-	6,114,862
1861	-	-	-	-	-	-	6.434,919
1862	-	-	Exhibition	-	-	-	6,046,242
1863	-	-	-	-	-	-	6,324,696
1864	-	-	Limited Liability	-	-	-	6,884,937
1865	-	-	-	-	-	-	8,137,753
1866	-	-	-	-	-	-	8,999,713
1867	-	-	-	-	-	-	9,422,742
1868	-	-	-	-	-	-	10,392,253

BELGIUM.

Year							Amount
1840	-	-	-	-	-	-	£880,286
1841	-	-	-	-	-	-	1,066,040
1842	-	-	-	-	-	-	1,999,490
1843	-	-	-	-	-	-	984,650
1844	-	-	-	-	-	-	1,471,251
1845	-	-	-	-	-	-	1,479,058
1846	-	-	-	-	-	-	1,158,034
1847	-	-	-	-	-	-	1,059,456
1848	-	-	-	-	-	-	823,968
1849	-	-	-	-	-	-	1,457,584
1850	-	-	-	-	-	-	1,136,237
1851	-	-	-	-	-	-	984,501
1852	-	-	-	-	-	-	1,076,499
1853	-	-	-	-	-	-	1,371,817
1854	-	-	-	-	-	-	1,406,932
1855	-	-	-	-	-	-	1,707,693
1856	-	-	-	-	-	-	1,689,975
1857	-	-	-	-	-	-	1,727,204
1858	-	-	-	-	-	-	1,815,257
1859	-	-	-	-	-	-	1,479,270
1860	-	-	-	-	-	-	1,610,144
1861	-	-	-	-	-	-	1,925,852
1862	-	-	Exhibition	-	-	1,828,622
1863	-	-	·	·	-	-	2,107,332
1864	-	-	Limited Liability	-	-	2,301,291
1865	-	-	·	-	-	-	2,935,833
1866	-	-	·	-	-	-	2,861,665
1867	-	-	·	-	-	-	2,816,481
1868	-	-	·	-	-	-	3,149,709

The returns of Belgium show no positive increase until the Exhibition year, 1862, and from that date they have continuously advanced.

Having now so far analyzed the returns of the various countries in connection with which our exports have most distinctly grown, and which, when taken as a total, may be said to represent the gross amount of our increased returns, it becomes necessary to take the gross yearly totals, and see how far the increase—the increase manifested by them—coincides with the existence of the causes thus laid down.

It will be necessary to refer to the fact that from 1840 to 1849 there is no marked growth of trade. There is large variation, but no defined increase. But it may be as well to notice, that a small increase year by year may be allowed as the mere result of the growth of population all over the world. For the same reasons that we are necessitated, by the increase of our population, to import continuously increasing quantities of corn to feed our people, so will the centres of our commerce increase in their demands, through the increase of the populations by which they are surrounded and which they supply. This may be taken as a cause that is always in operation; and which will, in all probability, act with greater force year by year. But such an influence will not produce sudden bounds of trade, similar to those which our returns continually show; so that, whilst admitting the cause, as being at once distinct and permanent, it does not form one of that group which has reared our past commercial success.

Passing from the consideration of this influence, we have those special causes that manifest themselves, and which have been already referred to, in examining the returns of individual countries. But we have yet to consider how far their value is manifested when the totals of our commerce are passed in review. In looking over our exports, certain indications manifest themselves very clearly. Our trade from 1840 shows no marked advance, until the influence of the gold discoveries of Australia and California, combined with the mass emigration of Ireland, produced their effect. The next influence that

TOTALS OF OUR EXPORTS,—1840 to 1868.

Year	Event	Amount
1840		£51,406,430
1841		51,634,623
1842		47,381,023
1843		52,279,709
1844		58,584,292
1845		60,111,082
1846		57,786,876
1847	Discovery of Gold in California	58,842,377
1848	Mass Emigration	52,849,445
1849		63,596,025
1850		71,367,885
1851	First Exhibition	74,448,722
1852		78,076,854
1853		98,933,781
1854	Outbreak of Crimean War	97,184,726
1855		95,688,085
1856	Peace with Russia	115,826,948
1857	Indian Mutiny	122,066,107
1858		116,608,756
1859		130,411,529
1860		135,891,227
1861		125,102,814
1862	Second Exhibition	123,992,264
1863		146,602,342
1864	Limited Liability Act	160,449,053
1865		165,835,725
1866	Financial Panic	188,917,536
1867		180,961,923
1868		179,463,644

came into play was that of our Great Exhibition, assisted also by the reduction of tariffs in different parts of Europe. These were again followed by the outbreak of the Crimean war, and, on the incoming of peace, our export trade again rose through the influences established in France, Italy, Turkey, and Russia by the war itself. Our Indian mutiny once more taxed our energies, and the greatest dependency in the world passed from under the sway of a private company, to be ruled as an integral portion of our Great Empire. The steps deemed necessary to retain our grasp on India, in case of a second revolt, found its expression in the development of the railway system, and the larger infusion of English life into the army—these causes again combined to raise our export trade. With but little variation, our trade remained stationary for six years; and when it again bounded, the cause was apparent in the Exhibition of 1862, aided, as it was, a year or two later by the gigantic creation of fictitious capital; and, since that bubble has collapsed, our trade has once more ceased to grow.

No reference has been made to that energy of character, which has everywhere developed our commerce, and which has made us the traders of the world; such reference was not necessary, as the question before us was, What were the special causes that had produced the rapid growth of our export trade? For the same reason no reference has been made to the capacity for trading that each nation may possess. The power to purchase must be assumed as an existing fact before any trade can be carried on; and so far as the government of states develops or retards the internal life of a country, it was foreign to the purpose now in view to investigate the question: but some illustrations bearing upon this matter are pointed out in consideration of the future influences of India.

We have now arrived at a point where it will be well to

look over the principles enumerated, and see how far they are trustworthy. The conditions connected with trade have been traced through three phases. First, on the broad principle that must underlie all trade—the simple principle of knowledge ; knowledge of goods themselves, knowledge of the people who sell them, and the gradual advance of civilization and its associate, the railway system. In the second place the individual action of special causes such as War, Exhibitions, Emigration, and Capital have been traced through those countries' returns, which more or less clearly represent the bulk of our increased trade. And in the third place, the totals of our exports have been viewed as totals ; to see how far they correspond with the principles laid down. The answers in each case appear to be the same : and the results seem to be connected as cause and effect.

GENERAL STATISTICAL SUMMARY.

	1840	1868
France	£2,378,149	£12,633,721
Italy	1,560,338	4,980,210
Egypt	79,063	6,068,569
Turkey	1,164,386	8,137,686
Russia	1,602,742	4,260,721
China	524,198	8,498,966
India	6,023,192	21,211,343
Australia	2,051,625	12,071,435
United States	5,238,020	21,410,184
Holland	3,416,190	10,392,253
Hanse Town	5,408,499	19,320,647
Belgium	880,286	3,149,769
Japan	—	1,106,069
68 other Countries and Possessions	21,034,742	46,222,071
Total Exports	£51,406,430	£179,463,644

The total of our export returns appear under about 82 headings, of that number the above 14 have been selected as representing not only the most important, but the most characteristic, of our customers; the remaining 68, which are enumerated in the Board of Trade returns, are included here under the general heading, "Other Countries and Possessions." The effect of this arrangement is largely to increase the special amount under the heading, although it still remains relatively small; the variation it shows between 1840 and 1868 having been equalled by the amount of variation exhibited by the United States at different years during the same period. In order that this may appear on the surface, the figures are subjoined to show the relative differences.

Amount of Exports to 68 Countries and Possessions.		Amount of Exports to the United States of America.	
1868	46,222,071	1866	28,499,514
1840	21,034,742	1842	3,528,407
Difference	25,187,329	Difference	24,971,107

CHAPTER III.

OUR FUTURE TRADE.

It has been wisely said, that the value we derive from the past is the teaching it yields for the future; and therefore the sketch of the causes that have developed our trade will be of value only if they enable us to decipher the probabilities that surround our trade in the future. The questions that everywhere surround us, and press with an increasing force, as day follows day and week follows week, is, Whither are we drifting? How comes it that the natural reaction has not yet come? In the past all other panics righted themselves rapidly, why not this one? Such are the questions that are everywhere uttered, until they become wearisome by their very sameness. The assumption that runs throughout them all, is, that there is a natural and inevitable power in trade to right itself. The warnings that speak through our commercial statistics from 1815 to 1840 are either unknown or ignored. The terrible trials incidental to long continued commercial stagnation, which made themselves felt in the past, are forgotten; and the only grave warnings that come to the surface are those daily increasing bankruptcies, which tell of slackened trade and increased competition. It will be necessary, for our purpose, that we keep close to our question, and watch how the causes of the Growth of Trade, when carefully traced out, can help us to elucidate the probable conditions of our future.

If the reasoning advanced in the last chapter be correct, the rapid growth of our past trade may be reduced to the following causes:—

First.—The growth of population and civilization all over the world.

Second.—The influence of emigration in connection with the discoveries of gold.

Third.—International Exhibitions.

Fourth.—The action of war as developing new relations with other countries.

Fifth.—The opening of new ports of trade, and the reduction of import duties.

Sixth.—The influence of capital.

We have now to consider which of the causes will continue in force without assistance; which of them we can stimulate; and which of them are likely to cease. It will also be necessary to bring into view the causes that operate against trade generally and our own trade in particular; such, for instance, as high tariffs and increased competition; and, when these are all fairly before us, we shall have a clear view of the question we have to decide.

With reference to the first cause, it may be fairly assumed that it will continue. The inhabitants of the world are ever on the increase and, as our commerce is world-wide, it must, from this one cause, be ever on the growth. We may also add to this, as an element inalienable from it, the gradual advance of civilization and education, both of which act as stimulants to trade, through the influence of increased knowledge and increased requirements; necessarily including in these the continuous development of the railway system, and its adjunct, the telegraph.

With reference to emigration, the whole tendency of events is to foster its increase. Not only has the desire to emigrate become very widely spread, but it is rapidly growing, and will be still further quickened by the gradual increase of labour in proportion to work. The totals of our emigration returns show a decrease since 1863, arising, no doubt, from the increased demand for labour at home, that characterised the years 1864, 1865, and 1866; but, as that demand has ceased, and as we have no probability of its resuscitation, the mere pressure, that will be exercised by the agency of want, will necessarily develope emigration. The capacity that this power possesses to aid our future trade is more specially detailed in the chapter headed " Emigration."

With reference to future Exhibitions, it may be said, that the more clearly the results are appreciated, the greater will be the care used to bring them into action, and to make them worthy of the purpose for which they were originally designed. That they have produced a large extension of our trade in the past seems beyond doubt, and that they possess an equal capacity for its development in the future, seems equally clear; the one question being, in what shape and under what circumstances they shall be called into action. With proper limitations there seems every reason to believe that we may anticipate from this cause a powerful influence in the development of our future trade. It will be obvious that the success of any Exhibition is more or less dependent on the mode in which it is carried through; if either from want of care, want of interest, or want of judgment, it be allowed to sink to the level of a private speculation, the power it would exercise over other countries would be proportionably reduced; if, on the other hand, the might of our national position be brought to bear, the success that would follow may be assumed as accomplished.

With regard to wars, they may be considered as almost things of the past: the power they have exercised has been specified, but their action in the future must be considered as very dubious: first, because the influence they possessed of causing nations to know one another is being rapidly superseded by other and more quiet means; and, secondly, because the whole weight of our influence and position is opposed to their recurrence; we having proclaimed to the world that our policy is a policy of peace.

With respect to the probability of the opening of new free ports, it must be remembered that the condition of Japan was entirely exceptional, and the circumstances that surrounded it will not probably occur again. The nearest approach to it is that of China; but the modifications introduced into our relations with that country since the war of 1860, leads to the belief that a more intimate commercial union may be anticipated between that country and our own. This tendency will be aided by the great emigration that has already made itself felt in Australia, and which is being organised for the Southern States of America. The results inseparable from a knowledge will follow, and those who return to China will carry with them associations and ideas that will fructify in the common interests of us all. Apart from the question of China, the pretension of isolation, so far as a country is concerned, can scarcely be said to exist. We cannot, therefore, anticipate any aid in our commercial future similar to that given to us, by Japan and the opening of its ports.

With respect to the reduction of tariffs, the tendency in Europe is evidently to bargaining, something after the manner of the Cobden Treaty, rather than the enunciation of Free Trade doctrines such as we have made. Whilst referring to this question, it may be considered whether it is not very questionable policy for us, in the present state of our labour market, to largely reduce our own. There is a time for everything; and the time for modifying our import duties does not appear to be peculiarly that of the present. Amongst a large section of our artisan class, there is a feeling that the reduction of any import duty exposes some particular trade to an increased competition—an opinion that no one who has watched the action of the

Cobden Treaty can for one moment doubt to be correct. It therefore becomes a grave question, whether it be wise, in the face of our present manufacturing difficulties, to make any change. The total results of the Cobden Treaty, when considered by its action on our trading population, are not of such a character as to justify us in proceeding further without very careful scrutiny.

We have yet to weigh one point which will very largely affect our export trade : and that is, the present course of policy pursued by the United States of America. The question is, whether it is probable that the United States will reduce or change their tariff? Our imports at the present moment are so heavily taxed as to naturally check our trade ; and, considering the peculiar ties of our relationship, there is probably no one cause that would so immediately increase our export trade as the removal of import duties from our goods entering America. It is well, therefore, to see what probability exists that the duties will be reduced or repealed.

It has been asserted, that the conditions that surround the customs of America are analagous to those that surrounded our own customs immediately preceding the change in our tariff ; it is therefore considered probable that the duties will immediately be reduced. In the next place it is asserted, that " Leaguers in New York and Boston are actively " disseminating the principles of Free Trade ; and it cannot " be doubted by any, one who is acquainted with the facts, " that, as soon as the task of re-construction is completed, " Free Trade will be the great question in the United " States." This may be so, and the result may be in accordance with the principles, but the reasoning does not appear to be satisfactory.

The assumption, that there is any tangible ground of comparison between the existing conditions of England and those of the United States, is so far removed from the ordinary laws of common sense, that it seems scarcely to require answering. England is a country so over populated, that she is absolutely dependent upon foreign trade to find food for a large portion of her people. America is a country where a great expanse of territory is still virgin soil, and which would, under proper cultivation, feed an almost indefinite population. England was driven to the revision of her tariff to find work and food for her people. America, embracing as she does every condition of climate, and possessing every necessary mineral, could shut herself off from the entire world and still grow as a great nation. What point of comparison can there be, when the fundamental conditions of existence are so utterly removed the one from the other?

But there are also other questions, quite apart from this point of view, which it will be wise for us to keep in mind. The policy laid down by the United States is, that her tariff affords the readiest means of collecting a revenue; and, looking at the enormous expanse of territory and the obvious difficulties of collection incidental to remote districts, there would appear some reasons for the maintenance of such an idea. In this view they will also be supported by the whole of their manufacturers, whose interests are identical with its continuance; and, considering the influence that manufacturers have exercised on this side of the water, it does not appear probable that any change will take place in opposition to their wishes.

In the *Times* of Nov. 23, 1869, is the following, apparently from one who, whilst a Free Trader, yet recognises the difficulties by which the question is surrounded. " Occasionally the " Free Traders invade Philadelphia, the citadel of Protection, " and although they have not yet mustered strength enough " to warrant a public meeting, they placard the blank walls

"and fences with huge posters, disseminating the heretical
"doctrines. The Protectionists on their side are not idle.
"Their journals defend the principle, and on the heels of the
"Detroit Free Trade meeting, they held another in that
"city, advocating Protection, challenging their opponents to
"a discussion, and forming a Protectionist Society. They
"have the advantage of wealth, numbers, and the control
"of the dominant party. .... Both sides, therefore,
"are organising their forces for the struggle that is to begin
"in the next session of Congress, but which will never be
"settled until the re-admission of all the Southern members
"and the strengthening of the West by the increase of its
"members consequent upon the new apportionment, follow-
"ing the census of 1870, give the Free Traders the prepon-
"derance of numbers and a partial victory. The first
"congressional battle will be fought upon the question
"whether the American shipbuilders are to be relieved from
"the depression on their trade caused by the high tariff
"of imported shipbuilding materials. In this no doubt the
"Protectionists will ultimately be beaten; but the interests
"of the different sections of the country are so diverse that it
"is scarcely possible for the Free Traders to gain a complete
"victory. The tariffs will never be any higher, but it will
"be some time before any material reduction can be secured,
"the present Congress being thoroughly Protectionist.

"Bills increasing the tariff, according to intelligence
"from Washington, are prepared there for introduction into
"the House as soon as the session begins, although their suc-
"cessful passage, after the fate attending similar measures at
"the last two sessions would seem almost hopeless. The wool
"interest, the cotton manufacturing interest, the iron and
"steel interest are all making loud lamentations about ruined
"trade and successful foreign competition, in order to raise
"a popular sentiment in favour of a further screwing up of

"the duties on these articles." . . . In the same letter, when referring to the opinions held by the President, he adds the following: "Mr. Kelly says that the President showed "that he had been studying the subject, and spoke particu- "larly against abolishing the duty on bituminous coal, as "such a step would take from the revenue a large amount "annually. . . . Mr. Kelly then went on to explain "his views on the tariff, recommending as the best plan to "put all articles of raw materials which America does not "produce on the free list, and to reduce the duties on articles "manufactured from raw materials which do not come into "competition with American productions; while the duties "should be advanced on all imported articles which can be "produced and manufactured in this country. With these "ideas Mr. Kelly says the President expressed concurrence, "and said he thought such a plan would simplify the tariff, "and afford the kind of protection needed to foster and "encourage home industry."

It is also well that we should have before our minds the opinions enunciated by Adam Smith, who, when speaking of Protection, says ("Wealth of Nations," Vol. II., pages 176—177) :—" By restraining, either by high duties, or by "absolute prohibitions, the importation of such goods from "foreign countries as can be produced at home, the monopoly "of the home market is more or less secured to the domestic "industry employed in producing them. Thus the prohibition "of importing either live cattle or salt provisions from foreign "countries secures to the graziers of Great Britain the "monopoly of the home-market for butchers'-meat. The high "duties upon the importation of corn, which in times of "moderate plenty amount to a prohibition, give a like advan- "tage to the growers of that commodity. The prohibition of "the importation of foreign woollens is equally favourable to "the woollen manufacturers. The silk manufacture, though

"altogether employed upon foreign materials, has lately
"obtained the same advantage. The linen manufacture has
"not yet obtained it, but is making great strides towards it.
"Many other sorts of manufactures have, in the same manner,
"obtained in Great Britain, either altogether, or very nearly
"a monopoly amongst their countrymen. The variety of
"goods of which the importation into Great Britian is pro-
"hibited, either absolutely, or under certain circumstances,
"greatly exceeds what can easily be suspected by those who
"who are not well acquainted with the laws of the customs.
"That this monopoly of the home-market frequently gives
"great encouragement to that particular species of industry
"which enjoys it, and frequently turns towards that employ-
"ment a greater share of both the labour and stock of the
"society than would otherwise have gone to it, cannot be
"doubted. But whether it tends either to increase the general
"industry of the society, or to give it the most advantageous
"direction, is not, perhaps, altogether so evident."

And although Adam Smith goes on to show that, as a broad principle, protection is unwise, yet, for the immediate purpose for which protection is now used by the Americans, the authority of the great founder of political economy can be adduced in support of the present tariff.

Beyond both these reasons, there is one that will weigh both long and heavily with the leading minds in the United States, viz.:—the large revenue yielded by the present tariff and power it thus affords the Government to reduce the war debt. There is no doubt that the most influential citizens of America, ardently desire to pay off their debt, and they will cling with great tenacity to any system, short of direct taxation, that will aid them to carry such a desire into effect. To many minds it is a question whether direct taxation could permanently maintain itself in America; and whilst any system exists that is at once productive and less onerous, there seems little reason to believe that a change will take place. The same remarks will apply, with modifications, to the great majority of the States of Europe, for throughout the whole of the issue now raised, this broad question runs—if the import duties now levied by the various countries of Europe were removed, by what means could a revenue be produced at once so certain and so little felt? and if so—why should they reduce their import duties? It is very necessary that we should endeavour to change the habits of thought in which most of us live, so as to take a fair view of the subject from a foreign stand point. We are so habituated to regard all these matters from the influence they have upon ourselves, as to ignore the fact, that the conditions, which are pressing necessities to us, may be a matter of small importance to other countries. With us the question is, how can our commerce be made to grow? How can we improve trade? How can we make other countries do that, which, whilst it is good for them, is also specially important to us? We say this, so much and so often, that there is ever a tendency on our part to become one-sided in our mode of viewing these questions. It would be difficult to show that the changes of tariffs suggested by many political economists are compatible with a ready equalisation of taxation in those places. Whilst this is the case, and we have keen discussions in our own land, as to the value of free trade itself, it is unreasonable to expect that foreign countries will adopt the policy which is still so vigorously challenged, where its teachings have been the most unflinchingly carried out; we must therefore come to the conclusion, that any modification of existing tariffs, sufficiently large to stimulate trade vigorously, must either be abandoned altogether or looked upon as very improbable.

With reference to any large action of Capital in the immediate future, it would appear that this also must be regarded as dubious. The rude shock to which all confidence has been subjected, combined with the glaring effrontery and utterly reckless swindling, developed in connection with our recent monetary collapse, is both too strong and too painful a lesson to be readily forgotten. Capitalists will prefer looking at their money to losing it; and they will either invest it in securities that are unequivocally sound, or allow their money to lie idle. It remains yet to be seen how long such a course is possble, but it is so at present, and will in all probability remain so for some time to come.

We have now passed over the various causes that have developed our trade in the past; and have found that amongst them those appear probable to aid us in the future, are:—the natural growth of population; the influence of emigration; and the general rise of civilization all over the world. All these causes are general causes, the operations of which, whilst very definite, will yet be very moderate, and we may therefore look forward, in the future under existing circumstances, to a very regular, but very gradual increase of our trade:—an increase which, at the largest calculation, could not be presumed to be in any sense equal to the necessities of our increasing population. We have yet to consider the counteracting influence of competition.

We have hitherto concentrated our attention on the causes that will develope our trade; but, to arrive at an accurate estimate, it will be necessary to view closely one cause, that threatens to operate with great force in the contrary direction, and that force is Competition. To say, that the greater portion of Europe is entering into direct competition with our leading manufacturers, is to assert that which is generally accepted as an established fact; but, in order to place the question in a clearer light, it will be better for us to take one or two distinct trades and follow them through the various influences that are at present acting upon them; for that purpose, and because they are our leading manufactures, Cotton and Iron have been selected.

So far as the mere quantities go, our cotton trade shews no material change. what we were doing in 1866 we are doing to-day; we hold our position, and no more. But the signs of increased competition are everywhere around us. It is asserted that Belgium cotton goods are being sold in the Manchester markets. It is undoubted that the cotton goods manufactured by Germany, France and Switzerland, are also imported into our country and that the imports are on the increase.

The figures being 1866 - 1,130,931
1867 - 1,185,287
1868 - 1,285,766

The increase as shown by these figures is not large, but it would appear to be definite. The totals here given would be of small moment except as indicating the capacity of foreign countries to compete successfully with ourselves. Beyond these, we have to remember that America is at the present time entering fairly into the race. It was lately announced that in one state alone, that of Tennessee, twenty-three mills had been erected, and it will be seen from the returns that the amount of cotton reserved for America's own manufacturers is continuously on the increase. Beyond this, the whole condition of American society would appear to point to a great growth of their cotton trade. The influence of her import duties will necessarily stimulate her home trade, and the natural advantages of climate, soil and position, all point the same way. If we add to these, the development of her railway system, the infusion of Northern blood into the Southern States, the immigration of the Chinese coolies, who are at once steady, patient, and tractable, we have combined a series of causes that may at any time produce a formidable and permanent rivalry. It is difficult to see why America should not eventually lead in the cotton trade; cotton is not only naturalized to her soil, but that which is produced is unquestionably the best in the world. She has machines equal or superior to our own, and the skill that has made our manufactures famous are leaving our shores by multitudes to find a new home there. If, then, she has material, skill and machinery, what are the reasons that should prevent her out-rivalling ourselves?

The circumstances connected with European competition are also significant. In Dr. Ure's well known work on cotton manufactures, reference is made to various Continental states, the particulars of which are here given.

A comparative view, given by Messrs. Rössingh and Mummy, of the importance of cotton manufactures in several different countries two or three years since, estimated the number of spindles working:

In Switzerland, at	1,250,000
In Austria, at	1,500,000
In France, at	3,250,000
In England, at	21,000,000

These numbers, however, are scarcely an index of the state of the cotton works in those countries at the present date.

Since 1845, Switzerland is stated officially to have quite superseded, in the markets of Germany and Austria, the yarns of Great Britain. In 1830, that Republic had in operation 400,000 spindles; in 1840, 750,000; in 1850, 950,000; and in 1860 about 1,250,000, the number having more than trebled in thirty years.

Before the breaking out of the late war, the manufacture of cotton in the Russian Empire was progressing with extraordinary activity. The number of spindles exceeded 350,000, producing annually upwards of 10,800,000 lb. of cotton yarn. The barter trade with the Chinese at Kiachta stimulates this branch of manufacutres in Russia, as the article of cotton velvets constitutes the leading staple of exchange at that point for the teas and other merchandise of China. In former years this article was supplied almost exclusively by Great Britain, but the Chinese prefer the Russian manufacture, and hence the steady progress of that branch of industry.

The cotton manufacture is rapidly increasing in Russia. It is scarcely more than thirty years since the first spinning mill was erected, and now it has 350,000 spindles in full activity, which produce more than 300,000 poods of yarn (10,800,000 lbs.).

The amount of cotton imported into Belgium in 1855, was of the value of 13,500,000 francs, and in 1856 there was an increased import of about 2,500,000 kilogrammes over the preceding years. The export of mixed cotton and woollen and cotton and linen goods has tripled in the last ten years, and Belgium now exports to, and contends successfully in the markets of North and South America with the great manufacturing countries.

The illustrations here given all point one way; and with the teachings derived at once from America, France, Belgium, Germany, and Switzerland, they seem to bear out the force of that reasoning which asserts that the principle of competition in our cotton manufactures is rapidly growing, and it will require all our skill, care, and attention to hold our own in the future. We are suffering from a too rapid success; the very grandeur of the fortunes realised in Manchester and elsewhere has drawn the attention of manufacturers all over the world to the philosopher's stone of cotton-spinning; and the result is, not only have we over-built ourselves, but other nations have given distinct evidences of their intention of contesting the race with us in our own markets, and there seems but little reason to doubt that in the future the competition in our cotton manufacture will largely increase.

The same, in a more modified sense, may be said of iron. In the latter case we have certain natural advantages which will be difficult to nullify: the quantity and quality of our iron ore, its contiguity to coal, the enormous organisation, and the large skill of our manufacturers themselves, all aid in maintaining this branch of our trade; but there are indications that the competition will even in this be very keen. Of late years Belgium, France and Prussia have entered largely into competition with us, in contracts for foreign orders; and the cost of shipment and transit in the case of all bulk iron goods materially aids their efforts. Not only is this true with reference to our foreign trade, but the same results have been produced in our home market; rails, engines, and machinery having been supplied by Prussian, French, and Belgian firms to our English consumers. In a note to Mr. Thornton's work " On Labour" are some remarks which are germain to the present consideration of this question and which are here subjoined.

" There is some reason to apprehend that the limits within " which unionist exactions ought in prudence to be restrained, " have already been in some cases overstepped. The importa-" tion into Hull of doors and window-frames from Stockholm, " the order from Russia of 40,000 tons of iron obtained in " 1866 by a Belgian firm in opposition to English competition, " the contract with the Dutch Government for rails wrested in " the same year by a Liége house from English ironmasters, " the fact of Belgian rails having been laid down on the East " Gloucestershire Railway, and of there being French locomo-" tives running on the Great Eastern line—these, after every " abatement of their significance that can be suggested, are " still ugly symptoms, which our unionist workers in wood " and iron cannot wisely disregard. I have seen it some-

"where stated (by Messrs. Creed and Williams, if I recollect
"rightly) that the order for 40,000 tons of iron, alluded to
"above, involved wages to the amount of £500,000."

We have now before us the general mass of facts that affect the probabilities of our future cotton and iron trade. It would have been easy to have extended the illustrations further, but these trades have been selected as representing not only a large proportion of ours export, but also as having been characteristically our own; they may, therefore, be considered more or less typical, and the reasoning that is true of these will be true also of others. The whole result appears to point decisively to the conclusion, that, under existing conditions, we have no right to anticipate a further large development of our future trade.

CHAPTER IV.

POPULATION AND FOOD.

In the last chapter an endeavour was made to trace out the probabilities bearing upon the growth of our future trade. It now becomes necessary that we should follow out the conditions that surround the question of Population and Food, as it is not possible to form a clear conception of the difficulties with which we have to deal, unless the facts connected with this portion of the subject are brought fairly before us.

At different times the effect, that excessive population may have upon the well-being of society, has awakened keen and animated discussion, notably so in the case of Malthus and those who follow the same class of thought; but the fundamental error, which appears to underlie all such discussions, is the attempt to elevate into an abstract theory that which is essentially a practical matter of fact. Throughout the whole of their argument, more or less definitely, the assumption runs,—that the world is already peopled;—that our knowledge of nature is complete;—and that the capacity of production through science is exhausted. Yet if there be any points absolutely clear they are,—that the world is not peopled;—that our knowledge is not complete;—and that science is not exhausted. It would, therefore, appear unwise to predict the future conditions of the world or to set limits to its capacity for human life. The mathematical formula that asserts the progresssve rate of population, but denies the same force to our food, altogether ignores the broad fact that life is as indefinitely expansive in the corn plant as in man, and that the law of progressive increase that governs the one governs also the other. To meet this by pointing out the practical difficulties that surround the indefinite development of food immediately changes the whole question to a mere matter of every day life; and we no longer discuss the abstract problem, but the practical conditions by which we are surrounded.

So far as the question refers to the immediate present, the world is not half peopled. The vast tracts of land in Asia, Africa, Australia and America that have yet to be be brought under the influence of modern cultivation are so enormous as to remove the whole question into the remote future, or into the changeful arena of metaphysical speculation. It may take long ages before the world is fully peopled, even under existing influences, and according to our present ideas; but to venture to limit either the power of science or the changes that may be evolved in that vast future is to assume a position that no ordinary reasoning can warrant; to attempt still further to deal with facts, circumstances and conditions, of which we can have no possible data, appears to be a mere waste of time, whilst practical difficulties remain around us. One illustration bearing upon the possibilities that surround the whole question may here be given, as showing how facts crop up, and how utterly wasteful all speculation must be, on a ground so shifting as that of human food. In Stuart Mill's "Political Economy" we have the following:—

"There is one contingency connected with freedom of "importation, which may yet produce temporary effects greater "than were ever contemplated either by the bitterest enemies "or the most ardent adherents of free-trade in food. Maize, "or Indian corn, is a product capable of being supplied in "quantity sufficient to feed the whole country, at a cost, allow- "ing for difference of nutritive quality, cheaper even than the "potato. If maize should ever substitute itself for wheat as

"the staple food of the poor, the productive powers of labour
"in obtaining food would be so enormously increased, and the
"expense of maintaining a family so diminished, that it would
"require perhaps some generations for population, even if it
"started forward at an American pace, to overtake this great
"accession to the facilities of its support."

But although the abstract question of population and food may be regarded as an intellectual gymnasium, yet from time to time cases arise in various parts of the world, when, through the force of circumstances, population becomes more dense than the land is capable of supporting, and when the practical question forces itself on our notice, and demands a solution. Such has been the case in Ireland, and such is the case in England to-day. In Ireland, we all know the result. We know how the people clung to the land, with a passionate intensity that poverty only increased; how, in spite of all warnings, the population grew and grew, sinking lower step by step, until the barest existence, sullenly eked out, was the utmost that could be hoped for. Denser and denser became the population, miserable and yet more miserable became existence, until at last they stood ever on the verge of famine. Under such circumstances the future was not difficult to foresee; the time was sure to come when starvation would set in, when, by the mere force of numbers, life would crush life out. It came at last: the potato blight fell upon the Irish crops, and the people died by thousands. An eye-witness thus describes it (Trench's "Realities of Irish Life"):—

"The crop of all crops, on which they depended for food,
"had suddenly melted away, and no adequate arrangements
"had been made to meet this calamity,—the extent of which
"was so sudden and so terrible that no one had appreciated
"it in time—and thus thousands perished almost without an
"effort to save themselves.

"Public relief works were soon set on foot by the Government. Presentment sessions were held, relief committees organised, and the roads were tortured and cut up; hills were lowered, and hollows filled, and wages were paid for half or quarter work—but still the people died. Soup kitchens and 'stirabout houses' were resorted to. Free trade was partially adopted. Indian meal poured into Ireland; individual exertions and charity abounded to an enormous extent—but still the people died. Many of the highest and noblest in the land, both men and women, lost their lives, or contracted diseases from which they never afterwards recovered, in their endeavours to stay this fearful calamity—but still the people died. We did what we could at Cardtown, but though the distress there was far less than in most other places, yet our efforts seemed a mere drop of oil let fall upon the ocean of misery around us— and still the people died!"

How clear the warnings had been, is testified by "Wade's History of the Industrial Orders," published in 1842, in which he says:—"The potato diet of the Irish is a principal reason that famines are so frequent and dreadful among them. The national subsistence depends on a single root, and if the crop of that fails, there is no other substitute to which they can resort. A wheat-fed population may, in the event of scarcity, obtain supplies of corn from other countries; but a potato-fed population, with wages to correspond, could not purchase the aid of foreigners, and if potatoes could be obtained, they are too bulky a commodity to be imported on an emergency. How different the state of a people, when bread, and meat, and beer, form the chief food of the labourer! Here, there is scope for retrenchment in a period of scarcity. From wheat, the working-man may temporarily resort to cheaper food—to barley, oats, rice, and vegetables. He has room to fall; but he who is habitually

"kept on the cheapest food, is without a substitute when
"deprived of it. Labourers so placed are absolutely cut off
"from every resource. You may take from an Englishman,
"but you cannot take from an Irishman—no more than from
"a man already naked. The latter is already in the lowest
"deep, and he can sink no lower; his wages being regulated
"by potatoes, the staple article of his subsistence, will not
"buy him wheat, or barley, or oats; and whenever, therefore,
"the supply of potatoes fails, he has no escape from absolute
"famine—unless he help himself, as the Irish do in dearths,
"to nettles, sea-weed, and sour sorrel, the last of which was
"found in the stomach of one poor creature who perished of
"hunger. Whatever has been the cause, the consequences
"of the number of labourers outgrowing the demand for them,
"have been deplorable. All inquiries respecting Ireland
"concur in representing the number of the people as exces-
"sive, and their condition as wretched in the extreme. Their
"miserable cabins are utterly unprovided with anything that
"can be called furniture; in many families there are no such
"things as bedclothes; the children, in the extensive districts
"of Munster and the other provinces, have not a single rag
"to cover their nakedness; and whenever the potato-crop
"becomes even in a slight degree deficient, the scourge of
"famine and disease is felt in every part of the country. The
"competition for employment and the competition for land
"have rendered both wages and profits little more than
"nominal, and both peasant and farmer are engaged in a
"constant struggle for the bare necessaries of life, without
"ever tasting its comforts."

The condition here depicted was that which existed previous to the outbreak of the dread famine of 1846. Since those days a great change has crept over the land; the Ireland of to-day is not the Ireland of thirty years ago, for, despite political discontent and social criminality, despite religious differences and secret organizations, her whole position is probably higher than it had ever before reached. This fact is testified by the investments in savings' banks, the increase in the value of farming stock, and in the generally progressive character in the value of land itself, the last the most decisive test of advancement. These great changes have been produced by the exodus of her people, which has diminished the population by one-third, and in short, reduced it to that number which the land can feed. The tale tells itself in the comparison of the population returns in 1845 and 1868.

The year 1845 the numbers were   8,295,061
    1868   ,,   5,532,342

the smaller number now being fed by the same means and from the same land as the larger number were in 1845. If emigration should still further continue, the result will be, that the state of Ireland will still further improve; but even under existing circumstances it has now only to produce food for two where it had to produce it for three; a problem simple enough for all of us to understand.

The condition produced in Ireland from over population has been chosen as an illustration of a general principle, because it was one near home, and one also with which we are all acquainted. The case was one where the people were fed from the land, and from the land alone; manufactures and commerce, as we understand them, had no place in Irish life. But, with some differences, we can press this teaching still more closely home; for our country also is over populated. England, more emphatically even than Ireland, cannot feed her own people; but the condition with us has been changed by the fact that, by our commerce, we have made ourselves a part of the entire world, through the creation of an export trade. It was the one channel open to us, and we availed ourselves of it. What seed time and harvest are to other countries, that our export trade is to us. It represents the fruition and garnering up of the stores by which one-half of us are fed. It represents also that portion of our harvest which has grown to meet the wants and supply the food for an ever-increasing population. When it slackens or ceases to grow, as at the present time, the warnings of destitution and discontent become everywhere manifested, because the people increase whilst their work does not. If in the open race our export trade permanently ceased to grow, the results that fell upon Ireland would also fall upon ourselves, with this difference—our Saxon thrift and foresight would prevent the full force of the calamity, and we should struggle through our difficulties, and find a home elsewhere. But how absolutely our export trade stands to us in the position here indicated will be best appreciated by following out the facts that can be shown to have existed in the past, and by our having before us what England and Wales can do towards the food of the people.

It has been said that we cannot feed our people by the produce of our own land, and this condition has grown upon us very rapidly. Less than a century ago, we not only fed our entire population, but exported food to other lands; since that date, although our country has been brought more largely under cultivation, and farming has risen to the position of a *quasi* scientific pursuit, and, as a consequence, the amount of food produced has been enormously increased; yet the fact still remains the same—we cannot feed our own people. How gradually, how stealthily, but how inevitably this has been so, statistics will most readily teach us; and they teach it in a manner that admits of neither equivocation nor doubt. In order that the case may be simple and complete, the growth of population is placed side by side with our imports and exports of corn.

POPULATION AND FOOD.

	Imports. Qrs.	Exports. Qrs.	Population.
1700—1709		1,047,026	6,186,815
1710—1719		1,045,949	6,252,427
1720—1729		1,044,960	6,217,861
1730—1739		2,767,130	6,168,099
1740—1749		2,995,591	6,244,533
1750—1759		3,127,164	6,528,193
1760—1769		1,384,661	6,936,970
1770—1779	431,575		7,363,640
1780—1789	233,502		7,914,703
1790—1799	3,216,095		8,724,213
1800—1809	5,747,528		9,513,111
1810—1819	6,550,466		11,004,612
1820—1829	8,146,679		12,903,059
1830—1839	15,082,607		14,724,063

During a considerable portion of the term here taken we were carrying on a large trade in corn, so that the usual returns of our imports and exports do not exhibit at a glance the actual state of the case; but, in order that the subject may be simplified, the imports and exports are deducted from one another, and the net result is here given. Each return represents the totals of every successive ten years.

It will be seen on looking at these figures that from the time that our population (England and Wales) exceeded seven millions we began to import corn, although the amount of the importation is too small for some time, to indicate more than the possible variations incidental to good or bad harvests; but, no sooner does our population exceed eight millions, than each successive increase of population is met by increased importations of corn. So clear and definite is this, that it may fairly be said that, under the then existing mode of life in England, and farmed as our land was then farmed, we could feed about that number. Since that time the yield incidental to the increased and improved cultivation has largely augmented, so that the actual amount of food producible is probably equal to the requirements of eleven millions of our people under the existing conditions of life.

But in order that this may be quite clear, it will be wise to take the actual amount of land under cultivation for the production of corn, and compare with it the amount of corn produced, as testified by the amount of home grown corn sold at the different towns of the United Kingdom, and shown by the Government returns. To prevent any misunderstanding, it will be well that the whole of the area of the kingdom, and the purposes to which it is appropriated should be placed clearly before us. For that purpose we can refer to the Government Agricultural Returns, which are here subjoined, as also some remarks bearing indirectly upon the question.

	Years.	England.	Wales.
Total Population	1868	20,451,233	1,198,144
Total Area (in Statute Acres)	—	32,590,397	4,734,486
Abstract of Acreage:— Under all Kinds of Crops, Bare Fallow, and Grass	1867 1868	22,932,356 23,038,781	2,415,139 2,503,646
,, Corn Crops	1867 1868	7,399,347 7,499,218	521,404 547,873
,, Green Crops	1867 1868	2,691,734 2,585,019	138,387 128,299
,, Bare Fallow	1867 1868	750,210 799,739	86,257 83,720
,, Grass:— Clover, &c., under Rotation	1867 1868	2,478,117 2,070,638	300,756 328,232
Permanent Pasture, not broken up in Rotation (exclusive of Heath or Mountain Land	1867 1868	9,545,675 9,703,884	1,368,329 1,415,327

"An increased interest may be taken in returns re-
"lating to the agriculture of the country if the annual
"addition to the total number of consumers of food in
"Great Britain be considered. In round numbers, about
"240,000 persons are annually added to the resident
"population in Great Britain. The additional wheat sup-
"ply required for that number at an average of six
"bushels per head, amounts to nearly 180,000 quarters,
"which, at an average English yield of 28 bushels per
"acre, represents the produce of upwards of 50,000 acres,
"and of a much larger acreage at a lower rate of pro-
"duction."

The statements here made are no doubt true, so far as the yield of the acre is concerned in certain very favoured localities, such as the fen portions of Lincolnshire; but it must be remembered that both in the Northern and Southern counties of England the cultivation would not produce a yield in any sense approaching the amount here named. Taking the average, and looking at all the circumstances, it may be doubted whether more than a quarter and a half, or some slight fraction beyond, could be assumed as being generally correct, a fact readily understood when the imperfect cultivation, bad harvests, and poor land are taken into consideration. This opinion is borne out by the returns of wheat, oats and barley of home growth, of which the quantities as sold during ten years are here given. It may be necessary to point out, that the returns of the amount of corn sold, are fuller 1840—1849 than they are at later dates, and the comparison as to acreage under cultivation has been obliged to be taken as late as 1867, as earlier reliable returns do not exist; and even those now taken are exceedingly imperfect, but it is probable that they are sufficiently accurate for the purposes now sought for.

Acreage in 1867 under cultivation for Corn was 7,399,347

1840	Qrs. of Home Grown Corn sold	-	8,156,855
1841	-	Do.	-	8,345,106
1842	-	Do.	-	8,869,950
1843	-	Do.	-	10,289,722
1844	-	Do.	-	10,280,444
1845	-	Do.	-	11,135,681
1846	-	Do.	-	10,867,809
1847	-	Do.	-	7,639,081
1848	-	Do.	-	8,824,446
1849	-	Do.	-	7,404,884

Average yield, 9,182,297 Quarters

It will thus appear that the average of acres under cultivation may be assumed to be at least seven millions, whilst the average produce sold does not much exceed nine millions of quarters; if we allow a large portion as being retained for home use, so as to bring the total produce up to ten millions five hundred thousand quarters, the result will be that which has been already stated—viz., a yield of one and a half quarters to the acre, or a capacity to feed about eleven millions of people.

It will be necessary to note that the standard of living is on an average much higher at present than it was a century ago, and we must, therefore, recognise that some proportion of our improvements in agriculture has been absorbed by that cause. But making all such allowances, it may be said that we can feed about the number stated above; and this estimate is still further borne out by the food we import, and which is equal to the requirements of the other half of our population—the total number being 21,642,577.

The returns of our imports of corn for the last three years are here subjoined, and when they are reduced into detail they yield about 1¼lbs of bread to each individual of a population of more than ten millions, and when the varying conditions of life are kept in mind, such as extreme youth, extreme age, sickness, debility, destitution, poverty, jails, workhouses and hospitals, &c., such quantities per head would appear to be a full allowance.

	1866.	1867.	1868.
	cwts.	cwts.	cwts.
Wheat	23,308,615	34,888,369	32,894,073
Wheat meal	4,972,280	3,592,919	3,098,022
	28,280,895	38,481,368	35,992,095

In addition to these imports of wheat and wheat meal, the whole of the quantities returned under the headings, Peas, Beans, Barley, Oats, Indian Corn, &c., &c., have been intentionally omitted, although they appear in the returns as corn food. It may be observed that several kinds are largely used for human food; such as oats for oatmeal, barley for groats, peas for many kinds of cooked food, and Indian corn for a variety of purposes, but the figures defining what portion is used for brewing, what for distilling, what for human food or what for animal food, are not given in detail and probably do not exist, so that a precise judgment cannot be formed, although the broad facts are clear and distinct; and they point out that the imports of food are larger per head than the quantity which has been taken in the calculations above.

If these estimates be correct, the result that follows is, that, since the close of the last century, the bulk increase of our population has been fed through the assistance afforded us by the increase of our export trade, and however great may have been our apparent successes in connection therewith, they have all been necessitated by the demand for food. With us it was not a question whether our export trade should grow in a greater or lesser degree; our position was this, that, if it failed to grow, we must either emigrate or starve. What efforts have been made and what results have followed will be best testified by a comparison between the amount of our export trade at the present time and at that earlier date when we could feed ourselves :—

   1770, £10,013,803   1868, £179,463,644

Or, in other words, the amount of our exports are eighteen times as great now as they were then. At the present time the mere variation of the returns from year to year is larger than the total of our exports at that earlier epoch. But at that time our commerce represented the exchange of our surplus productions, and the fancies that sprang from accumulated wealth; to-day our commerce represents the necessities of life, and the means by which our people are fed.

In order to follow this out, it will be necessary that we should have before us the actual relation existing between the growth of our export trade and population, and this will be best exhibited by the following table. The year 1840 has been taken as the starting point, as it was from that date the previous comparisons in connection with our export trade were made. The returns are taken at intervals of five years.

	Exports.	Population.
1840	51,406,430	15,730,813
1845	60,111,082	16,739,136
1850	71,367,885	17,773,324
1855	95,688,085	18,829,000
1860	135,891,227	19,902,713
1865	165,835,725	20,990,946

But the relation that our export trade bears to the people is, not the relation to the population as a whole, but to that portion which may be described as our surplus population, being that portion over and beyond what we can feed by the produce of our own land. Assuming the number we can feed to be eleven millions, the actual condition of our export trade with reference to population will then be represented as follows:—

	Exports.	Surplus Population.
1840	51,406,430	4,730,813
1845	60,111,082	5,739,136
1850	71,367,885	6,773,324
1855	95,688,085	7,829,000
1860	135,891,227	8,902,713
1865	165,835,725	9,990,946

It will be seen that our later returns show a relatively large increase; this is partly explained by the general increase of wages, and partly also by the improvements in machinery, which would swell the total amount of the returns, without increasing the demand for labour. The rise in price of the raw material—such, for instance, as cotton—is another cause why our trade might be larger in amount and not larger in reality. With these allowances and explanations the gross increase of our returns keeps pace with the increase of our surplus population.

Viewed in the light here indicated, our present condition would appear to be the natural sequence derivable from known facts. If in 1866 when we were at the height of our commercial prosperity, our population was not only equal to all demands that were made upon it for the purpose of producing the requisite amount of manufactured goods, but if at that time, we had a large mass of able-bodied pauperism lying absolutely idle, it was sufficiently clear that labour was then in excess of all demands. Since that date our trade has receded and is not to-day equal in amount to what it was then, and yet our population has grown to the extent of six or seven hundred thousand people. The results that follow appear to be inevitable. If we have more people to feed and less means of feeding them, it will be quite obvious, why we have the destitution, misery, and pauperism that now surround us, and why, under existing circumstances, it is so continuously on the advance. It would appear to be equally inevitable, that so long as our population continues to increase and our export trade does not grow in proportion, so surely will the misery that is now so great, deepen in intensity.

It would have been easy to extend these facts, but the desire has been to place the relation that population bears to food in a clear light, and then allow it to tell its own tale. Through all classes of figures, through all classes of facts, through all classes of life, its teachings may be found. It speaks to us through the Registrar General's Returns, as day by day we see those figures mount up; it speaks to us through that cry of sorrow and want that may be heard throughout the land; and it speaks to us through that ever widening field of human sympathy, that toils to alleviate misery, but toils utterly in vain. The stream of poverty that is diminished to-day swells into mendicity to-morrow, and threatens to overwhelm us by pauperism the day after; and still the cries increase and the struggle deepens. Above all there rises the never ceasing question:—How is the difficulty to be met, and how are the people to find both work and food?

CHAPTER V.

LABOUR.

In the last chapter an endeavour was made to trace out the points bearing upon the question of Population and Food; but Labour, Pauperism, and Emigration, are so linked and entwined with it, that the reasoning which relates to the one shades off imperceptibly into the other. Press any one of these subjects vigorously, and the others will spring to the surface; track them all home, and they will be found bound to the same centre, they are the radiating lines of the same general cause. In the present chapter it is proposed to follow the question of Labour so far as its influences can be shown to affect our present circumstances.

At the outset it will be well to state, that there is no intention to discuss the many abstract questions that are connected with the subject; such as, the probable future of labour, the value of machinery to human progress, the relationship it bears to co-operation, and so forth. All these questions are exceedingly valuable; but the point aimed at here is the practical solution of existing difficulties, for the grandest reach of abstract thought is of little use unless it blends its teachings with the necessities of every day life.

The question now before us is, What are the circumstances, at present in force, that tend to affect the demand for labour, and whither do they lead in the future? With this end in view, it will be necessary to trace out the causes that influence our agricultural pursuits, our home and foreign trade, as well as keeping in view the effect that machinery now has, and probably will have, upon them all.

The whole condition of agricultural labour reduces itself into the simple question, of the amount of land under cultivation, and the amount of labour that is required to cultivate it, according to our present standard. It is of course possible to conceive a state of things in which agriculture may be carried to a much higher development than it is at present, but we must remember that the practical question is, at what point can agriculture be made to pay, and it is idle to expect it will be carried beyond. Under the pressure for food that has existed now for nearly a century, all the more available and valuable lands have been appropriated; and although it may be anticipated, that in consequence of the vigorous demands which will probably be made upon the Government, some portions of the waste lands of the kingdom will be brought under cultivation, yet such an effect will be too slow and too small to materially affect the present question. We may therefore assume that so far as consumption of labour is concerned the demand in connection with agricultural requirements is amply supplied at the present time.

But there are new causes now rising into existence which will tend to make the existing supply of labour in agricultural pursuits more than equal to all requirements; and one prominent cause is the introduction of machinery. Within the last twenty years steam ploughing, steam thrashing, steam hoeing, and steam drilling, have passed from the domain of speculation into that of practice, and the result is, and will necessarily be, a gradual diminution in the demand for that manual labour, which had been previously employed in doing the work.

It is very often assumed that the introduction of steam into any industry in reality creates labour. In certain trades this is true; for instance, when the introduction of steam-power so cheapens an article that the demand for it is enormously increased; or in the case of a newspaper, where the question of rapid production is the very element of its existence, and, as such, an adequate supply can only be produced by th aide of steam. Under such circumstances the introduction of steam machinery creates a demand for labour instead of reducing it. But it is impossible to apply the same reasoning to agricultural pursuits; a plough, whether drawn by horses or driven by steam, will only plough the land, and the element of time, which makes steam the necessity in a newspaper, does not exist with reference to land. If the land is not ploughed to-day it can be ploughed to-morrow; but the newspaper that is not printed to-day is not printed at all. Steam thus becomes a necessity in the one case, but not in the other. If therefore steam is used in agriculture, it is used primarily because it does work both cheaper and better. We may therefore naturally anticipate that as the value of steam in agricultural operations becomes better appreciated, it will be more extensively used, and, as a consequence, the demand for labour will be further lessened.

The general result here indicated is borne out by the population returns, for it is found that the actual numbers employed in our agricultural pursuits are less now than they were formerly, and this has taken place notwithstanding the influence of the Enclosure Act, which has already added 504,391 acres to the general area under cultivation since 1845. This diminution in the demand for labour in our agricultural districts is proved by our population returns. In 1851 the number employed was 2,011,447; in 1861 the number employed was 1,924,110; showing a diminution of 87,337.

Another reason may also be given. The introduction of railways has had the tendency to draw people from the country into the large towns, and thus reduce the labour seeking employment in the more rural parts. Still one further reason may be added, the marked tendency to large instead of small holdings of land, the effect of which is to economise the expenditure of labour; but, whatever may be the exact causes, the result is clear. Our farming to-day, although over a larger area and more carefully attended to, is carried out with less manual labour than was previously required. And it seems difficult to conceive any circumstances that will permanently stay the increasing tendency to the reduction of labour in connection with our agricultural pursuits. It would therefore appear probable that we must anticipate a diminution in the demand for labour so far as agriculture is concerned. Let us now pass to the consideration of the conditions that surround our home requirements.

It is impossible to avoid seeing that another portion of our home requirements is dependent upon the condition of our export trade. When our export trade is good, when orders are large, and when as a sequence manufacturers are prosperous, the whole condition of the country improves, and labour is better paid. But the opposite condition is also true; when trade is stagnant, manufacturers cease to be busy, and depression settles down upon our home trade. This is our condition to-day; and it appears probable, for the reasons which have already been given, that it will be still worse in the future. We may therefore accept as a broad proposition, that the growth and development of our export trade is a large and permanent cause affecting the condition of our home trade, either for prosperity or adversity.

Entirely beyond this portion of the question, there are several reasons which must be considered before we can come to any reliable conclusion; first among these must be the recognition that during the last thirty or forty years we have passed through a series of circumstances that have made large demands for labour, but which cannot, under the ordinary conditions of life, again occur. During that period we have founded, constructed, and developed the entire of our railway system, and we have done this at an enormous cost of time and money. Short connecting lines here and there, a new station at one place, or a new junction at another, will be continuously occurring; but the system, as a system, is built and founded, and will not, therefore, require the amount of labour in the future that has been required for its construction in the past.

These facts will be more clearly developed if we bring definitely before our mind the amount of capital invested in our railway system, and picture to ourselves the quantity of labour that has been required to bring it to its present position. In 1866 the amount invested was £481,872,184, of which sum more than 200 millions had been expended since 1853. We may readily conceive what a large influence the expenditure of this capital has had upon the whole labour market of the country, for we must remember that a greater portion of this money was employed in paying for labour,—labour of constructon, labour for engines, rails, carriages, &c., &c., and although in the future a certain amount will still be required to effect the changes incidental to all large operations, and a further amount must be allowed for wear and tear, yet the greater proportion of all such labour will be required no more.

The same general remarks will be found applicable to many of the changes that have taken place in London. A simple enumeration of some of the works which have been carried out within the last few years will best illustrate this; a list of some portion of such works is here subjoined:—

H

Main Drainage Works,
Thames Embankment,
South-Eastern Junctions and Stations,
London, Chatham, and Dover Stations,
Midland Do. (King's Cross),
Metropolitan Railway,
Westminster Bridge,
Hammersmith Bridge,
Blackfriars Bridge,
Holborn Viaduct,
City Improvements, &c., &c.

All these works may be regarded as permanent works, not requiring renewal for some centuries; and yet these works have, by a series of causes, been condensed into ten or twelve years, absorbing during their construction a very large amount of labour, and liberating the same quantity of labour on their completion. If works of equal magnitude and of a similar character do not require to be constructed in the future, how is the labour to find employment?

We may press the question still further home by remembering that the enormous expansion of our past commerce has called forth an equal development of factories, workshops, and machinery. So much has this been the case that the constructive capacity of our country has grown until it has reached a level equal to its greatest demands. The full force of this will appear when we remember that the existing conditions of our factories are at least equal to an export trade of 200 millions per annum, and our present trade is 20 millions less than that amount.

We are prone to ignore or forget the fact that the workshops of the country do not require continuously rebuilding. We have built in the past, because—with few exceptions—our commerce has grown continuously in the past, and we needed more mills and more workshops to produce the goods for our ever increasing trade; but when that commerce ceases to expand the demand for new buildings and new machinery must cease also.

The conditions that surround the great bulk of the people will also make themselves felt one way or the other. If trade be prosperous, the general status of the people rises, and this influence spreads by bringing into play dormant capital through the increased demand for improved modes and circumstances of living. This result was evidenced in our time of prosperity from 1851—1861 by the more than proportionate increase of houses that were built in comparison with the increase of population. The detailed statistics are given at page 91, "General Report of Census, 1861." But when circumstances change, when the pressure of want falls upon the people, the demand for new houses ceases, and this cessation in the demand for building enacts fresh want by the mass of labour which is thus thrown out of employment.

We have yet to consider another power whose influence is not only permanent, but is rapidly gaining ground, in the sway it is exercising over labour—that power is steam machinery. Notice has already been taken of the influence it is exercising upon agricultural labour in England, but the reasons that have been thus urged apply with still greater force to manufactures. At the present moment, as well as in the past, the whole weight and force of the best inventive brain of the country is, and has been, directed to the production of machinery that will economise labour; the qualities of rapidity and certainty of production being in another form mere economy of labour. To what an extent this force of invention acts may be judged of by the fact, that in cotton machinery alone, from 1,200 to 1,500 patents have been taken out for improvements. Every conceivable modification has been worked out, many that are utterly useless have been tried, but, as a final result, our cotton machinery is almost self-acting. Nothing can be more beautiful, more delicate, more finished, or more perfect; but, as a final result, there is an enormous economy of labour.

The same general principle is found to run through all manufactures. Machinery and processes for the economisation of labour are everywhere adopted. At the present time, under the existing system of intense competition, an invention that successfully realises the specified conditions, creates a large fortune to the holder of the patent : the consequence is, that the whole sweep of thought relating to manufactures is devoted to the production of improvements. One case may be selected that will illustrate this. A few years ago it was announced that iron could be converted into fine quality of steel by the simple process of casting. This assertion, which was at first ridiculed, has since become an accepted truth and is now known as the "Bessemer process," and some of the facts connected with it are thus stated in Roscoe's "Spectrum Analysis :"—"I may mention in connection "with these different carbon spectra, the application of spec- "trum analysis to the important branch of steel manufacture, "which has been introduced and is well known under the "name of the Bessemer process. In this process five tons "of cast iron are in twenty minutes converted into cast steel. "Steel differs from iron in containing less carbon, and by "the Bessemer process the carbon is actually burnt out of "the molten white-hot cast iron by a blast of atmospheric "air." It will be obvious that the mere result of this invention is, to make steel available for purposes usually requiring iron; such, for instance, as our lines of rails, &c., &c. : and as the wearing power of steel is very largely in excess of iron, the effect is to reduce the demand for labour in this branch of industry to the difference existing between the two materials.

But the illustration here given might be multiplied indefinitely. Inventions exist for sawing and polishing stones, making doors and sashes, moulding bricks, &c., &c., and, in fact, there are in all large branches of manufacturing industry, inventions of some kind or the other for the economy of labour, and this tendency is ever on the increase. One more illustration is here added, which will tell its own tale :—" *Pall Mall Gazette,* June 4, 1869.—A labour dispute " of considerable magnitude threatens the East Worcester- " shire district of the black country, the principal seat of the " wrought nail trade. In the neighbourhood of Bromsgrove " about 2,000 nailers are already on strike, and the dis- " content is so great in the villages around Dudley and " Stourbridge that it is feared the workpeople in those parts " of the district will be induced to join the movement. Mass " meetings are being held in Bromsgrove, at which the half- " starved but resolute nailers express their firm determination " to hold out. The wrought nail trade—on which some " 25,000 persons in this district depend for subsistence—has " been revolutionized by the introduction of machinery, and " in many departments the wages of the handicraftsmen have " been reduced to the lowest ebb."

Some few facts have now been given and it may be well, before leaving the subject, briefly to examine the results here indicated. It may be asserted that the whole force and value of machinery rest upon the economy it effects in labour. All railways, all spinning machines, all paper mills, &c., are based upon this one idea ; and as the force of thought connected with manufactures is continuously directed towards this end, and as competition increases, individual men are induced to make still more vigorous efforts to succeed in the race of life, and the result is that new ideas and new inventions spring into existence, and, as a consequence, the demand for labour is still further lessened.

In the past the tendency to reduce employment by the introduction of machinery has been held in check, by the enormous development of our export trade. The mere fact that we now export 130 millions per annum beyond what we exported in 1840, will explain how it was that our increased population found employment, whilst our improved machinery largely reduced the demand for labour, for the labour, then liberated, became rapidly absorbed by the demands incidental to the growth of other branches of industry. This explains our condition in the past, but it altogether fails to explain how the requirements of our future are to be satisfied, except by a rapid and continuous expansion of our export trade. As our labour market stands to-day, our position is this, we have to find employment, not only for our increasing population, but also for those workmen who are thrown out of work by the reduction in the demand for labour, the result of improved machinery.

Men seem afraid to admit this truth; they appear to shrink from the acknowledgement that the introduction of machinery lessens the demand for labour, yet it will be idle to blind ourselves to the fact that machinery, as a broad principle, does, to a great extent, supersede labour; and if it failed to do this the machinery would be worthless. Such a recognition is quite compatible with the definite acknowledgment that machinery is not only valuable but absolutely indispensable; it produces evil results only when we allow, as we have allowed to-day, the other conditions of life to overlap one another. The slightest investigation would show that even as England is placed, it would be utterly impossible that the great bulk of the people could either be clothed, fed, or housed, as well as they now are, but for the extensive use of machinery; yet this very recognition is embraced in the assertion that machinery lessens the demand for labour, not only as a temporary influence, but as a permanent result.

We have now briefly travelled over the points that affect labour through the existing means being more than equal to our requirements, and the consequent certainty that the skill which was required to build railways, bridges, workshops, &c., will not in the future be required to the same extent as in the immediate past. We have also traced out how the whole tendency of machinery is to lessen the existing demand for labour, and to lessen it both rapidly and definitely. We have now to examine one more influence that acts upon our labour market before we are in a position to form a sound judgment, and that is the relationship of the labour market of Europe to ourselves. We all accept the statement that ease and rapidity of communication have a direct tendency to equalise existing conditions; and this is true of labour as of all else. The various strikes, riots, &c., &c., both at home and abroad, induced by the introduction of foreign workmen into our own land, or from the introduction of our own workmen into foreign lands, will be an illustration of the effect of this influence. We have therefore briefly to consider, is it probable that the labour market of the Continent can absorb any of our surplus labour, or is the tendency the other way?

To this it may be answered that the labour market of Europe is already full to overflowing. At the outset we are met by the pregnant fact, that Germany, Switzerland, Belgium, and France are keenly competing with us, in the various markets of the world; a valid proof that in all these countries, labour is in excess of its demands. Still more conspicuous are the facts that in Germany emigration to the United States, and in Switzerland migration over the whole of Europe are marked and permanent conditions of existence in these countries. In Belgium life is exceedingly dense; whilst in France the greatest efforts are made to keep down discontent by the various devices to stimulate trade, and by the creation of Imperial workshops; all these various efforts are made only because the population can find work by no other means. But amongst our French neighbours this question of excess of population over work has spoken out again and again. It peered through the embers of the First Revolution, and found its answer in the wars of the First Napoleon. It awoke the teachings of Fourierism, St. Simonism, Socialism, and Red Republicanism, all which gained heart and strength from it alone. The inequalities of life may give point and force to anarchy, but the key of sedition is to be found in the grasp of hunger. Looking, therefore, alike at the past and the present, labour in Europe would appear to be in excess of all demands, and the probabilities are that the Continent will send labour to compete with ourselves, rather than that they will be in a position to relieve us from our surplus.

Before leaving this question, it will be well to note the position of the existing armies of Europe. It is not necessary to trace out the evils that arise from great standing armies, but simply to mark their effect upon labour. At the present moment the number of men under military service is believed to exceed five millions. From time to time the enormous expense incidental to their maintenance, forces under consideration the question whether a general disarmament cannot be carried out; and although under the existing circumstances of political life, such a step must be considered impossible, yet a reduction will probably take place sooner or later. The creation of armies to their present magnitude has taken place within the last twenty years, and the effect has therefore been, that the labour market has been relieved to the total number of men thus absorbed. We have, therefore, to consider, first, what will be the effect if no war of magnitude should intervene,? and, secondly, what would be the effect of a grand reduction of the standing armies? In both cases the result would be the same : the overstocked labour market would be still further pressed by the surplus labour liberated from military service and the effect of such a step as a general disarmament it is impossible to foresee ; but it obviously differs from that which many of its most urgent supporters anticipate. A rapid disarmament in the face of a stagnant trade would not improbably manifest itself in wide spread revolution.

Looking, therefore, at all the circumstances connected alike with our home and export trade, the relation that we bear to the labour markets of Europe, and the very powerful influence that machinery is destined to effect in the future, it would appear to be inevitable, that the demand for labour in our own country is at present on the wane. Let us track out how this bears upon that question which is ever rising, and never answered—the condition of Pauperism.

CHAPTER VI.

PAUPERISM.

What is the future of Pauperism? Is it to remain the evil that it has been for so long, or has the time arrived when we shall be driven to face a great and growing difficulty by the mere weight of its pressure? The great mass of figures that stands before us as a menace—varying with the seasons, the march of epidemics, and the greater or lesser depression of trade rouse us from our lethargy, and challenge our reply. Are we to be content with tabulation, classification, and supervision? Are we to be content that this huge force of waste labour, degrading and degraded, shall remain for ever in the midst of us, accepted as a part of our normal life? or have we a right to demand that the question shall pass from the condition of more or less efficient organization into that of remedial statesmanship?

Nothing can be more clear than the one fact, that the Poor Law Board neither attempts, nor pretends to attempt, to deal with any of the broad questions that bear upon pauperism. It accepts and wields its position as a simple administrative power, limiting its range and scope of thought to planning schools, arranging nurseries, or erecting infirmaries. From beginning to end it is content with this position; it treats pauperism as an element of our social life, for the well being and training of which it is responsible, but responsible for nothing more. If pauperism increases or decreases it asks no questions. It supplies the existing wants, carries out the necessary detail, and leaves the rest to chance. To the ever-recurring questions, How is pauperism to be met? what are the causes from which it springs? why does it ebb and flow? the Poor Law Board affords neither hint nor suggestion—it is not its function. But the time is fast coming when the question will force itself before us by the mere weight of an ever increasing burthen, and will raise the broad issue; Are we to accept pauperism as an inevitable necessity, or are we to struggle on with an incubus that threatens to crush us? This is the question of which all other discussions are mere outlying points.

It is easy for men—even honourable and upright men, who do not feel the pressure of poor-rates—calmly to point out that the evil has been as great before, and has conquered itself. But to those who stand on the verge line of struggling life, inheritors alike of poverty and toil,—that huge class from which pauperism is fed;—to them the question is not one of balancing and weighing, but one of overwhelming and crushing necessity; to them the question rises up in its naked significance, when their home totters to its fall under the mere pressure of ever increasing rates.

There need be no evasion of the broad fact, it is the poor who feed the poor; it is in the pauperised districts where the rates mount up, and where pauperism is most bitter and the longest sustained; and it is in those districts where the load weighs most heavily. But if this were all, the mere reorganization and redistribution of our poor rates might meet the difficulty; but the causes lie far deeper: they lie partly in the fact that population is in excess of work, and in the still more important fact that the prospects of the future point decisively to the increase of this difficulty.

By some it is asserted that the causes of pauperism can be traced to imperfect education, drunkenness, epidemics, or bad harvests; and although all these influences are powerful as partial agencies, they are utterly unequal to explain the broad facts of the case, or to check those more potent influences that underlie the whole. If education were perfect, if drunkenness were extinct, if epidemics ceased to exist, and if bad harvests were unknown, there would still be some portions of our social life that would belong of necessity to the pauper class. No conceivable conditions can blot out the possibilities of accidents, imbecility, or disease; and no organization, however perfect, can struggle against those powers which spring into play when trade slackens, and employment is no longer to be found. We must, therefore, recognise, and accept whilst we recognise, that pauperism is an inalienable portion of all human society; and that the ameliorating influences of sanatary laws, education, and sobriety may reduce, but cannot extinguish, the evil.

But the teaching that stands up before us is, that pauperism, as we now understand it, is a thing of modern life, and that the mode of dealing with it which was befitting a state of society such as existed at the time of Elizabeth is useless for the changed conditions of to-day. The very enactment that was passed indicated a class who are now represented by our mendicants—the sturdy beggars who could work but who would not, those who had been fostered into idleness through doles at convent doors or church porches, those who lived, and were content to live, by beggary. To such a state of society the law that introduced the labour test had a substantial meaning. The enactment runs as follows:—" The churchwardens and overseers, with the con-
" sent of two justices, shall take order, from time to time, for
" *setting to work the children* of all such whose parents shall
" not, by the said churchwardens and overseers, or the greater
" part of them, be thought able to keep and maintain their
" children; and for setting to work all such persons, married
" or unmarried, having no means to maintain them, and
" using no ordinary and daily trade of life to get their living
" by; and for the necessary relief of the lame, impotent, old,
" blind, and such other among them being poor and not able

"to work. Thus it clearly appears this was an act for enforc-
"ing industry, not for encouraging idleness. No one was to
"be relieved, either child or adult, except, if able, by setting
"to work. The subsequent practice of granting money
"allowances, without equivalent labour, to able-bodied
"persons, and thereby creating a band of parish pensioners,
"was certainly never contemplated by the authors of this
"celebrated piece of legislation. . . . Between the age
"of Elizabeth and the present exists this important distinc-
"tion—the difficulty in the former was, as has been shown
"in the preliminary history of the industrious orders, to
"compel men to work; the difficulty is now to find them
"work to do. The idea of an able-bodied person willing
"to labour but unable to get employment, was never enter-
"tained by Lord Burleigh and his contemporaries. The
"object of their great measure was to meet the evil of
"idleness and vagabondage, which grew out of the decline
"of feudality. Hence I conclude that the obligation (if it
"exist) of parishes to relieve or find employment, for able-
"bodied paupers, has grown entirely out of the altered cir-
"cumstances of society, and that as these circumstances did
"not exist in the time of Elizabeth, the act passed in her
"reign could not have been framed to meet them."—WADE.

Let us consider what are the circumstances connected with the pauper life of to-day? and what course of action it is necessary to follow out? The first glance at the question indicates that there are three distinct classes of paupers:—

Those who cannot work;
Those who will not work;
Those who cannot find work to do.

Those who cannot work are composed of the deserted, the broken, the aged, and the helpless; the waifs and strays of life, those elements which are an inherent portion of every society, and which every society will accept the responsibility of maintaining without a murmur. But this element of our pauperism is the smallest part; and even the proportion it now bears to the remainder is due to the general condition of our overloaded labour market, for the pressure that tells upon the artisan tells still more upon those to whom he is the natural protector; and, the consequence is that a large proportion of those who are now reduced to seek relief would, under more favourable circumstances, be taken care of by their own friends.

The class that will not work the class which trades on our pity, infests us with letters, whines at our elbow, or loiters at the area gate, is being brought under the influence of mendicity laws, through the effort now being made to propagate societies founded on the system so ably and successfully established at Blackheath, through the agency of the Rev. Mr. Hart, and which aims at ridding us of shams by placing itself in connection with the parish; relieving exceptional cases by exceptional means, and having for its final aim the check of mendicity. We must not shut our eyes to the fact that this course of action will not reduce mendicity; it simply changes its place and character. The mendicity that is driven from Blackheath finds its outlet at Westminster, driven from Westminster, it infests Paddington; driven from Paddington, it goes elsewhere; and, if driven from all positions, it eventually comes back upon the rates as a part of our recognised pauper population. It may be, and possibly is, wise to force this result; but it is equally well to recognise what the end is that we eventually achieve. The effect here pointed out follows from the one fact, that able and efficient workmen are in superabundance in every trade, and whilst respectability struggles in vain to obtain work, mendicity has little chance of employment. The result, therefore, will be that if mendicity societies actually succeed, mendicity will sink either into pauperism or crime.

But even if mendicity were capable of being dealt with in its entirety, it would be but a small portion of pauperism. The class which is at once the largest, the most respectable, and the most difficult to deal with, is that class which seeks for, but cannot find, employment, and which represents not only the greatest number, but also that portion of pauperism which, under existing conditions is, and must be, steadily on the increase. It is curious to note how the tide of pauperism ebbs and flows, but still more curious to note how its ebb and flow are dependent upon the state of our trade. In order that the evidence may be clear, the last twenty years have been taken, and, on the assumption that our export trade represents the means by which our surplus population are fed, the comparison is here instituted between the expansion and contraction of our trade, and the increase or decrease of pauperism:

	Paupers.	Export.
1849	934,419	63,596,025
1850	920,543	71,367,885
1851	860,893	74,448,722
1852	834,424	78,076,854
1853	798,822	98,933,781
1854	818,337	97,184,726
1855	851,369	95,688,085
1856	877,767	115,826,948
1857	843,806	122,066,107
1858	908,186	116,608,756
1859	867,470	130,411,529
1860	851,020	135,891,227
1861	890,423	125,102,814
1862	946,166	123,992,264
1863	1,142,624	146,602,342
1864	1,009,289	160,449,053
1865	971,433	145,835,725
1866	920,344	188,917,536
1867	958,824	180,961,923
1868	1,034,823	179,463,644

In looking over these figures, it is perfectly clear that when trade expands, pauperism decreases; when trade contracts, pauperism increases. A large number of the class, who seek employment but cannot find it, come to the parish only when driven to it by want of work, and they pass from the parish books so soon as trade improves. There are two exceptions in the table which it will save trouble to explain—those of the years 1856 and 1863. In the year 1856 the influence of a bad harvest, combined with the reaction consequent upon the termination of the Crimean War, led to a great increase of pauperism. In 1863 the influence of the Cotton Famine, an event without parallel in the history of trade, made itself felt, and sufficiently explains the exceptional increase of our pauper returns.

This element of pauperism is gravely important because it represents a class that is reduced through the influence of circumstances which they cannot control. The magnitude of this portion of our pauper population will be best appreciated by some remarks made by Lord Houghton. Speaking in the house of Lords, April 17, 1869, on the question of pauperism and emigration, Lord Houghton said:—" What " are called the able-bodied poor considerably exceed 150,000, " that being an increase of 7 per cent. on the numbers in " 1867, whilst those numbers again were an increase of 6 per " cent. on the numbers in 1866. It is apparent therefore " that, notwithstanding the increase of wealth, pauperism is " steadily advancing." The numbers here given are equal to that of a large army, and since that date they have much increased, but even at these figures it will be quite apparent how great a proportion of the whole pauper class they must represent, when the children belonging to them are taken into account. If then this element of pauperism—that which seeks work but cannot find it—be as it would appear to be, the largest portion of our whole pauper class, any suggestion that attempts to deal with pauperism must deal with it through the relation it bears to labour, or by direct removal of the paupers themselves.

There is one phase of the question which is of grave importance and now presses itself prominently upon our notice: the tendency that exists to create a pauper class, through the influence of long continued relief. As facts at present stand, our every effort has a tendency to recoil upon ourselves; the relief that is given to-day, saps the self-sustaining energy of the recipient, and if long enough continued, destroys not only the inclination to work, but all sense of self-respect. The difficulties of this position are intensified by the fact that a large number of those, who at present rank amongst the pauper class, are driven to that position through the state of trade. The evils that this inflicts are twofold, not only is the *morale* of the class lowered, but the whole tone of thought in connection with pauperism itself becomes insensibly changed. It is impossible to feel the same pitying contempt for those who are driven on to the parish by the mere badness of trade, as we should feel for the idle and dissolute, who sink by their own want of principle. A feeling of commiseration, which is naturally awakened for the hard working man, overcome by circumstances, is thus gradually extended to the whole of the pauper class, and is aided by the utter impossibility of discriminating one from the other. Under these circumstances, and if long enough continued, the whole character of pauperism will change; and the brand of the pauper— in its present meaning—will pass away.

The gravity of this danger it is impossible to deny, and it is still further increased by the broad fact that we have in the midst of us a permanent population of more than one million who receive aid, and who live on from year to year, acknowledged by us, as an integral part of our national life.

It is impossible to believe that such a proportion of our population can permanently exist as paupers, without the moral influence of such a position eventually reacting upon our own thought. Such a result is already beginning to manifest itself in the criticisms of some portions of our daily press; and if this influence be strengthened by the element of misfortune now furnished by slackness of trade, we may anticipate a large development of the feeling. If the opinion but once gains firm hold, that pauperism is an evil to which the honest and hard working are equally liable with the careless and improvident, the check that is now imposed by a sense of self respect will exist no longer. The inevitable entails no disgrace: and the destitution that springs from causes we are powerless to control, brings no shame.

Amongst the other difficulties that surround pauperism, there is one that springs from the existence of a purely pauper class, those who are born from and belong to what may be called the pauper blood. There is no fact in physiology better established than the one which teaches that like produces like, the pauper begets the pauper, the taint, be it what it may, that runs in the blood, appears and reappears in spite of all training and all circumstances; manifesting itself time after time under conditions where it would be least looked for; exhibiting all the qualities of incompetence and recklessness; and the pauper, ever drifting back to the parish, quietly submits to his condition, and accepts it with contentment. This class is well known to all guardians, and may be regarded as the true pauper type. In striking contrast to this are the cases that from time to time occur where the child of a brave man's nature, nurtured though it may be in the very hot bed of pauperism, shows, as the force of life gains upon him, the thirst for freedom, and the willingness to maintain himself by labour; the typical child of the pauper makes his effort by the mere force of education, and, when these conditions are not all in his favour, gradually sinks back into the depths from which he had emerged. The importance of this portion of the question comes more clearly before us when we remember the large number of children that are born in the workhouse.

It is needless to say that a large number of these children are illegitimate. Born under such conditions, and reared amidst paupers, what is more natural than that the taint of the mother should reappear in the child? If the evil of indiscriminate alms-giving creates mendicity, what is the probability but that pauper children, reared as they are and passing out into life under the circumstances that created the first taint, must, sooner or later, return to the workhouse? The facts are so; for it is well known that a large number of pauper born children eventually come upon the rates.

Many see the outlet to this difficulty in the force of a larger education; but what education is so strong as the education of habit? the teaching from books, great as it undeniably is, cannot compete with the teaching of facts, and the first knowledge of a pauper child is the fact that he is a pauper amid paupers. The atmosphere that belongs to the outside world has no existence for him; the fierce play of individual energy that belongs to our struggling life comes to the pauper child only when he moves out from the system of which he is a unit, to take his place in the world. And the training that had reared him, considerate as it may have been, is still the training associated with pauper thought and not the one best fitted to give him that strength to struggle with those difficulties which are inseparable from his position. Some attempts have been made to meet this difficulty by the introduction of a system of "farming out," based on the idea that the teachings of life are more soundly inculcated by the children being reared amongst that class to which they naturally belong and to which they must revert when they have to earn their own bread. This system promises well, the one great advantage being that the child is brought up free from pauper association. But the difficulty connected with our pauper children is still increased by the tendency that exists to teach them the usual handicraft and trades, whilst skilled workmen are already in large excess, the consequence is, that their first start in life is hampered by the difficulties, inseparable from such a set of circumstances. Robust natures may struggle through, but feebler natures will sink back to the Union. It has therefore been urged that it would be wise to bring up some portion of pauper children to a knowledge of agricultural pursuits, with a distinct idea that their future lot will be best secured by emigration.

There is no doubt that the question of how to rear pauper children forms one large element of the responsibility of parishes, but, great as that responsibility is, it does not end there; the difficulty that presents itself in the future is one almost equally as great, for it is impossible to avoid, and it is senseless to slur over, the ever recurring question, how are they to live when they arrive at maturity? No doubt exists that every home occupation is full even to overflowing, and it is equally true that in every branch of trade the effort that is necessary to make a livelihood is at all times very great. How then are we to meet the position? The answer clearly is, to place the children in circumstances where a demand for labour exists, and where the largest advantages are offered for their future, both morally and physically, and there is no opening so befitting as that of emigration to our colonies.

Those who see in emigration a great means of lifting up our status as a people, and those who see in the same course of action an utter wasting of our strength, yet cordially concur in the testimony that skilled manufacturing labour in all our colonies is in excess; and all equally agree that the skill of the farm servant and husbandman is in demand. This one fact would seem to point out the wisdom of dealing with pauper children, by recognising that the colonies are their natural home, and by giving them such an education and trainng as will fit them for an employment for which the demand not only exists in the present, but will be much larger in the future. The objection that exists to the emigration of pauper adults does not exist to that of pauper children; the colonies absolutely reject the one, but would be willing to receive the other; and if, when children, these paupers be removed to fresh scenes, and planted amid fresh influences—if placed where the teaching to rich and poor is,—Help Yourself—the profound value of such circumstances it is impossible to over estimate. It may be urged that the expense would be unduly large, and one that a parish has no right to undertake; but it is exceedingly doubtful whether the cost would be at all equal to the permanent drain now made upon the ratepayers by the continuous call for the support of those who could support themselves. But entirely beyond all this, there rises the broad question whether pauperism cannot fairly claim government assistance for such a purpose. Such a concession would not be very large, nor is there much probability it would be refused, if the question were fairly brought forward.

We have now arrived at the point where emigration rises to the surface, and where a series of causes combine to point out its value; but we have yet to trace out the influence that mass emigration has had upon pauperism itself, as illustrated by our statistical returns. The condition of Ireland after the famine affords us this opportunity, and it affords it also, under circumstances exceptionally clear, and the teaching thus yielded is both marked and decisive. At the time of the famine, in 1846, the numbers were enormously large, but no returns were taken, the first being those in 1849, at which time a large reduction of the pauper population had already taken place, through the influence of state-aided emigration.

	Paupers.	Population.
1849	620,747	7,256,314
1850	307,970	6,877,542
1851	203,187	6,514,473
1852	171,418	6,336,889
1853	141,822	6,198,984
1854	104,604	6,083,183
1855	85,296	6,014,665
1856	72,247	5,972,851
1857	55,183	5,919,454
1858	49,308	5,899,814

It will be noticed that year by year the population decreased, and pauperism decreased in proportion. In ten years the mass emigration from Ireland had the effect of reducing the number on her pauper roll from 620,747 to 49,308, and the reduced number may be considered about the normal proportion that pauperism bears to her population, for since that date, with very slight variations, the numbers have remained the same. We have, therefore, this one fact, that in Ireland the effect of her great emigration has been to reduce her pauper population to one-twelfth of what it was, and to keep it at that position. This will be still further enforced by a comparison between the two countries. At the present moment, population for population, there are five times as many paupers in England as there are in Ireland. In England the proportion is nearly 1 in 20, in Ireland nearly 1 in 100:

1868	Population.	Paupers.
England and Wales	21,649,377	1,034,823
Ireland	5,532,243	56,663

One fact connected with Irish emigration, and the influence it has had upon pauperism, it is necessary to point out. The Irish emigrate in families—men, women, and children, old and young, all go together; whilst in England, the very opposite is the case At the present time English emigrants are represented by the youngest and most energetic portion of the population,—those who have sufficient foresight and sufficient courage to dare all risks, and seek to found a home for themselves elsewhere. They go alone; the ties of kinship, which form so strong a trait in Irish character, has little or no existence amongst this portion of our population, and the result is, they leave behind the aged and the feeble, who have to shift for themselves or come upon the rates. This difference in the class of emigration from the two countries goes far to explain the cause of the existence of one portion of our pauperism,—those who cannot help themselves—and to indicate how it might be avoided. It seems difficult to believe that we shall be content to allow pauperism the same latitude in the future as we have allowed it in the past. It seems still more difficult to believe that the power of emigration can longer be ignored as a means of reducing within moderate limits the great incubus of our pauper population. It is not intended to urge that the same amount of emigration is necessary for England as was necessary for Ireland, but the lesson is best taken at its worth, be the teaching what it may.

The question of emigration, as bearing upon pauperism and destitution generally, was discussed in connection with

Lord Houghton's motion in the House of Peers, and the opinions enunciated by men eminent alike by their ability and position was distinctly opposed to the furtherance of emigration even as a means of relieving the labour market. Lord Overstone said, " He wished their lordships to consider "seriously what was the evidence that this country was in "such a condition as to require that we should resort to an "extensive system of emigration. In his opinion all the "elementary principles which affect the social condition of a "country told a very different tale from that with which the "noble lord who brought forward the question sought to im- "press the House. He recollected that a few years ago the "noble earl, who was at the head of the Government, had said "to him, with a tone of surprise, that an eminent financial "authority had told him that our annual savings amounted to "£75,000,000, and had asked him if he believed the state- "ment to be correct. His answer was that he would have "stated the amount at a much higher figure, and subsequently "he had occasion to notice that all the ablest statisticians of "the country had put its accumulation of capital at some- "thing like £150,000,000 a year. Now, the capital of a "nation was its labour fund, and yet, with the enormous "accumulation of capital which he had just mentioned, we "were told that we must resort to every means in our power "for exporting our labour. . . There were two main causes "of distress and want of employment. First of all there was "what he might term local congestion, by which certain classes "in particular parts of the country were thrown out of work. ". . . . Another cause of distress was the periodically "recurring causes of commercial crisises; but he had always "maintained such events were the seed of expanding pros- "perity in the future." Earl Grey, after complimenting Lord Overstone, said, "He entirely concurred with him in believing "that the country was not, in the ordinary sense of the word, "over peopled. There was no excess of population beyond "what the country was well able to bear. . . . He main-"tained that to reduce the numbers of our working population "would be to take away the very sinews and strength of the "country." The Earl of Carnarvon followed in the same strain. These opinions have been quoted, not because of their force of thought, or accuracy of statement, but because they were found sufficient to silence the discussion, being considered absolutely conclusive by the House of Peers. Yet what in reality are the reasonings that carry so much weight, and what are the evidences advanced in support of the reasoning? The arguments advanced by Lord Overstone were the only ones in which any attempt was made to bring the subject home to ordinary minds, by appealing to plain facts and acknowledged principles, and it is worth while, not only on account of the gravity of the question itself, but also on account of the eminent position held by Lord Overstone, to examine carefully the general reasoning advanced by that nobleman in support of his assertion that there is no necessity for large emigration. Reduced to brief phraseology, the case may be stated as follows:—

1st.—That destitution was partial, being due to local congestion of trade, which would right itself.

2nd.—That our present depression was due to an ordinary commercial crisis, which, instead of being an evil, might be regarded as the condition from which would spring increased prosperity.

3rd.—That the profits of the country, formed the labour fund of the country, and as our profits were equal to 150 millions per annum, it was impossible to regard our present position in any other light than a mere passing disarrangement.

With regard to the first, if there be any facts clear, they are those that point out the very opposite of the position to that laid down; for instead of depression being merely local, it exists, more or less, all over the country and the cases of activity of trade are not only local and exceptional, but due to very special causes; the evidence of these facts are to be met with in the general discussion throughout the whole of the press, in the demand for free emigration and in the great rise in our pauper returns.

With regard to the second point, that the present is a mere commercial crisis due to over speculation, the answer is, that there is no case in our past commercial history, where the stagnation from a commercial crisis has been equal to that of the last four years, and this stagnation has existed in the face of an export trade, that is to-day, very much larger than it was ten years ago; our commercial panic produced large stagnation, but the endeavour to explain a series of compound causes by one passing influence fails, not because the principle itself is not true, but because it is only a small part of the truth.

No mistake is greater than that which assumes that mere commercial panics greatly affect trade ; when any such occur, the speculative few may be injured, but the real trade of the world remains substantially unaltered, for the great nations who buy our calicoes neither know of, nor care, for a financial panic; they eat, drink and are merry, whether it occurs or not; the power they possess to buy of us, and the power we possess to supply their wants, remain absolutely unchanged by the question of any panic. Beyond this it must be recognised that a commercial crisis is a result not a cause; a result not of over trading but of over production, and when that occurs in the sense that it occurs to-day, when we can produce not only all the world asks from us, but an amount of manufactured goods very greatly in excess of all possible demands under the existing conditions of life ; we thus have that which we have now, a great commercial crisis, permanent depression and long continued want. It is therefore unreal to explain a great phenomenon, like that of the present condition of our country, by reference to a commercial crisis that passed over our commerce nearly four years ago. The explanation is, the power of production is greater than the power of consumption.

Another point to which Lord Overstone refers, and on which he lays great stress, is, that as the profits of a country form its labour fund, and as our profits are enormously large, the demand for labour in our country must increase in like proportion. It seems very necessary to point out the grave error that runs throughout the whole of this reasoning. The assumption that labour will increase in proportion to our profits, is not only not correct but is opposed by the most common-place facts. It is quite true that profits do really form the labour fund of a country; but it is even more emphatically true that our country has long since passed the position when she could make use of her profits for the extension of her trade. The mere fact that on our Stock Exchange loans for every conceivable purpose, and from almost all the countries of the world, are not only now, but have for a very long time past, been taken up by our surplus capital seems a final answer to any question about the action of profits upon the labour market. A century ago, a demand existed for money to supply the various requirements incidental to wars, the growth of trade, and the springing up of our commercial relations all over the world; these causes demanded a large amount of capital, and as a consequence, our profits then formed a large element in the growth of trade; but, when these needs were satisfied, our profits had to find outlets elsewhere, and they have found them in the various foreign markets. Some part of the haziness of thought that surrounds this portion of the question is due to ideas promulgated by Adam Smith, who pointed out how the realised profits formed a fund which aided labour. This condition was true of his time, but the circumstances are so utterly changed that in our country to-day, instead of capital being required, it is already largely in excess; the difficulty at the present time being, not to find the capital, but to find the legitimate use for it. When therefore it is gravely in excess, what effect can the mere increase of that excess have upon the demand for labour or the growth of trade? Not only do these facts exist as now stated, but throughout the whole country our manufactories are all built, and the capital necessary to develope and carry them through is already in existence; what is now required for the present condition of our trade, is not the capital for the construction of larger powers of production, but the demand for the goods which our factories are capable of supplying. We must therefore except as altogether apart from the question any endeavour to connect the influence of profits with any direct increased demand for labour.

We have now arrived at the point where it is necessary to count up the whole of our results. Putting on one side all the minor questions of mendicity, &c., &c., the evidence points out that probably the largest portion of our pauperism is due, directly or indirectly, to the excess of labour over employment, or in other words, a large portion of our pauperism comes from want of trade; it still further points out how some portion of the residue of our pauperism is due to causes that are capable of being still further reduced by such means as the emigration of our pauper children, and by aiding in the carrying out a system of family emigration as distinct from individual emigration. We therefore stand face to face with these two conclusions, that a development of our trade will reduce pauperism, and that a large emigration will have the same effect. The question now before us is how can these two ends be accomplished so as to act with justice to all concerned.

The first question will be the condition of Emigration in its double aspect as a means for relieving our over loaded labour market, and as a means for developing our export trade; and, in the second place, the capacity that India possesses for the consumption of our manufactures, in both cases acting as a direct agency for the reduction of our pauperism and the elevation of our people. The conviction is gaining ground slowly, but definitely, that emigration is one great power for good; and beyond this arises the idea that the country needs not only a great emigration system, but one aided, developed, and controlled by government agency. The question is, how can this be carried through so as to aid the manufacturer, elevate the artisan, and reduce the rates? On its capacity to effect these three things depends the large value of emigration.

CHAPTER VII.

EMIGRATION.

EMIGRATION is a great law of the world; it was so in the past, it is so in the present, and it will be so in the future. Its teachings come down to us through the dim light of tradition, and the fuller light of history; and above the changes of dynasties or the wreck of empires its course moves on unchanged; whilst its influence has done more to mould history than the action of warriors or the efforts of statesmen, for it belongs to, springs from, and is a part of, that widest of all wide laws—the growth of population. Men must live: if the country yields an insufficiency of food, the common instinct of self-preservation bids them find a home elsewhere; and hence comes the great principle of emigration.

The need for its fulfilment is heavy upon us to-day; with every avenue of trade filled to overflowing, with destitution widely spread, with a giant mass of pauperism, with machinery lessening the demand for labour, and with a population whose increase is more than four thousand per week, the question rises before us in a form at once vivid and startling, and points out the gravity and necessity for such a step as large emigration. Many see and accept this conclusion; they recognise with an unwavering distinctness the aid that emigration can bring towards the solution of our present difficulties, and they crave with a great craving the opportunity to test its capacity. This is evidenced by the huge mass of people who crowd to every emigration meeting, by the testimony of working men's societies and by the appeals again and again brought forward asking for Government aid. These tendencies force upwards the questions why is aid refused? and in what relation should the colonies stand to the mother country?

The reasons for refusing Government aid are not difficult to find. They rest on the assumption that the necessity which would justify such a step does not now exist; they rest still further on a feeling, more or less widely spread, and more or less distinctly enunciated, that the removal of our surplus population would destroy the strength of the country. It should in justice be said that those who hold such opinions are quite removed from the position where the logic of hunger has the opportunity of speaking out. The refusal for aid rests also upon the belief that our trade will revive sufficiently to re-absorb our suplus labour; and, in the meantime, the compressibility of life, short work, poverty, rates in aid, and the workhouse, will carry the difficulty through in some way or the other.

By some it may be considered altogether unwise to raise these questions; but from beginning to end the discussion of these subjects is not a matter of free choice, they are forced upon us by the conditions of life that now surround us. If pauperism did not exist, if destitution did not exist, if starvation did not exist, it would not be idle but it would be wearisome to discuss the huge idea of a continuous mass emigration, fostered and carried through under government superintendence; but, when the question rises before us in the shape of ever increasing rates and ever increasing misery, and when it is pressed still closer home by the mutterings of socialism, and by open air discussions as to who are the rightful owners of the land, it is at once lifted out of the ordinary conditions of political life into that status when it must be dealt with, whether we will or no.

Let us suppose that Government aid be refused, let us

still further suppose that private aid is lavish, and through it an organization is brought into being to remove some portion of our surplus population; such a step can only temporise with the evil, and a year or two later it will have assumed a still greater proportion. The actual growth of our population for which there is no work and no prospect of work, is 220,000 per annum; can private aid grapple, or permanently deal with a problem so great as this? Beyond this it must be remembered that mere emigration, that is, the mere removal of the surplus population from our own shores to that of any other shore, will not solve the problem. Sooner or later such a course would produce evils, almost as great as those we now seek to remedy, at the points where our own people were landed: and we should thus not be grappling with the difficulty itself, but simply shifting it on to other places. It will be quite clear that any great mass of emigration directed towards any of our colonies, without previous provision being made for their reception, would eventually entail great destitution and misery. Besides this, it is obvious that such a course of action could not permanently maintain itself, for foreign countries and our colonies would very vigorously object to being treated in any such manner. We must therefore be prepared to face the absolute condition of the question that emigration has the double phase: the removal of our surplus population from our own shores, and the more or less direct preparation for their reception elsewhere. And the probability would appear to be, that we must ultimately accept a distinct system of colonization.

There are some persons, although it may be assumed not many, who will wrap themselves up in their own self-sufficient wealth and affect to ignore the gravity of our present position. Let them not be mistaken. The warning notes of danger rise high in the air and challenge the whole condition of our present social life, and if less evident are none the less real. Those, who know the under current most thoroughly, know, that discontent is deep, stirring and wide-spread, and that the angry outbreak, which now and then rises to the surface, is but the spark that springs from the fire of sedition which smoulders below. One thing is quite certain, men are not prepared to starve, and rates in aid will scarcely silence the awkward questions concerning the land which will be madly discussed, when want drives the teaching home. What those questions are, whither they tend and what they teach, may be gathered from open air speeches and socialistic discussions; whether right or wrong, they exist and will gain force, point and consistency from the pressure of want.

Emigration would modify, if not remove, all this. Our people are patient, hard working and long suffering; only show them how they can earn their bread, and hot political discussions will sink to the regularity and temperance of House of Commons debates. Let the contrary take place, let the recognition sink into the minds of the people, that political crotchets are considered of more importance than the lives or well being of the people themselves, and the education of political thought will grow with strange rapidity; no teacher like hunger and no harvest time of sedition so prolific as that of idleness and want. But beyond all this their rises the question, why should aid be refused? The logic that sees strength in myriads of people even though pauperised and starving, and would chain a population to our shores for which we have neither need nor work, is so utterly puerile that it needs no answer. The question stands up, clearly and distinctly in its two phases; on the one side there is hunger, desperation and danger, on the other a growing trade, an improving national life and hope for the future. The question is, which shall be chosen, and if chosen how chosen, and in what manner acted upon.

K

There can be little doubt which course will eventually be chosen; the press of life thickens every day, and the pressure of thought evolves more and more vividly the elements of the great problem of our future, and so soon as men grasp clearly and fixedly the broad fact that mass emigration is a great necessity, all the consequences that flow from that position will follow very rapidly; but it would appear to be wise before such a time arrives to recognise clearly what it is that has to be done. The first requirement that stands out is the necessity for creating a system of free passage to our colonies by Government aid; and the second requirement is, distinct arrangements with our various colonial authorities so as to ensure work to emigrants when they arrive at their various destinations. Around these two points a number of questions revolve, which it will be wise to examine.

One objection may, and probably will be, urged against such an idea. It will be distinctly said that it is not the place of Government to undertake any such arrangements, for by the ordinary law of supply and demand, things will right themselves. But what is meant by supply and demand? There are cases that from time to time rise to the surface where, from sheer pressure of want, all energy, all forethought, all hope is more or less crushed out. It may be asked, How can such people find for themselves a home elsewhere? How can those who know not where the bread of to-morrow is to be found find means to pay for emigration? They may be honest, willing, and hardworking, but they are powerless; they are so utterly beaten by circumstances, that there is no possibility of their being lifted up but by help from without. Leave them where they are, and permit the law of supply and demand to work its own results, and what will follow? Starvation, mendicity, and the workhouse. What they need is aid to lift them up and to place them where the struggle for life is less bitter. The argument that applies to the lowest of this class will, with modification, apply also to the highest. Many an artisan may possess the power to pay for his own passage to another country, but has no means to pay for those who belong to him, and if he avails himself of the advantages of emigration, he must go alone, and leave his wife and children as a burden to the parish. It is for these reasons we must recognise that aid is so imperatively needed; those who have the means and the will to emigrate need no consideration; they ask no questions, seek no favours, and carry their energy where they will. But for those who are so beaten down as to be utterly helpless, those who have no hope, no means, and no friends, to all such state aid must be given if they are to emigrate at all.

The question naturally arises, if aid be given, in what form should it be given, and with what intentions. It has been suggested by Lord Carnarvon that, however the problem may be worked out, the most prudent arrangement that is open to us is by means of loans to our colonial governments. Such a course seems at once simple and wise; but it will be necessary that a more decisive statement of the case should exist. If money be lent to our colonial governments it would appear necessary that it should be lent for a three-fold purpose: first, the benefit of the mother-country: by relieving the overloaded labour market, freeing us from some portion of our destitution and pauperism, and for the purpose of developing our commerce. In the second place, the benefit to the colonies by the influx of labour, the means for whose payment and use would be guaranteed by the money lent by the Home Government; and, in the third place, the benefit to the emigrant by the opening up of a new field for labour, in which the advantages would be all in favour of those who work.

It would seem only reasonable that any scheme of emigration should combine all these results, and also that the reasons on which the whole movement is based should be so clear that all persons could understand them. Differences of opinion will be sure to exist, but, in proportion as the absolute necessity of emigration becomes more and more evident, the difference will be that of detail, and not that of principle. It is also reasonable to recognise that, as England will have to bear the first brunt of the burden connected with any emigration scheme, the value the movement can have to her position and to her commerce should stand clearly in the foreground. The growth of our commerce is to ourselves an unconditional necessity, and the power that emigration posseses to effect this end is only beginning to be recognised even by those who take the largest interest in these questions. But, keeping these points in view, let us trace the idea through.

The great field of enterprise that is open to us, in connection with a widely spread and carefully nurtured system of emigration, it is almost impossible to realize, and the part that it is capable of playing in our future commerce has scarcely attracted the attention it deserves. The vast area of our colonial empire is to-day practically untouched, myriads of acres of land lying waste and useless, the natural mines of wealth of our future as soon as they are brought into use. The capacity they possess to feed an enormous population is recognised as an abstract fact—but very little more, and they are only considered in this sense when the prospect of widespread destitution forces the question to the surface, as is the case at the present time; but this mode of viewing the subject is at once spasmodic and fragmentary, and shuts out the condition of value that our colonies can be made to bear to our future commerce.

At the present time our colonies buy from us a large portion of our exports, about one quarter of the whole, and there is no substantial reason why they should not be made customers to an amount equal to the total of our present export trade with the entire world. This assertion may at first sight appear unreasonable, but let us examine the whole conditions of the question. At the present moment the probable total of our colonial population—apart from India—is about ten millions of people, and they are spread over a space equal to one quarter of the globe, located on the mere borders of our colonial possessions. It has hitherto been found that as these populations increase, either by the natural growth of population or by the increase of emigration, our exports increase in proportion, being checked only by high tariffs and the growth of their own manufactures. The result, therefore, resolves itself into this: that so soon as our colonial population has increased fourfold we may anticipate our exports will have increased in like rates. An illustration of this capacity for absorbing our exports was given by Australia at the time of the discovery of gold; a second was given at the time of the Californian gold fever; and it has already been pointed out in the chapter on the Growth of Trade, that there is a distinct connection between the mass of our emigration and the increase of our exports.

The reasons for this being so are very large. All new countries must purchase their manufactured goods from Europe or America and will continue to do so until they erect manufactories of their own. It is therefore obvious that the direct action of emigration is to increase our export trade. We have also to remember that the land which is valueless, whilst it remains untilled, creates wealth by the action of labour; and the ploughman, who is a burden on his parish in Hertfordshire or Somersetshire, or who migrates to the nearest market town to swell still further the poor rates there, rises into position and use in those parts of the world where the land requires his labour, and, as he thus rises in life he always becomes a larger purchaser of our home manufactures. The first essential of all trading is the capacity to pay for what is bought, and this power of payment, in any large sense of the term, must come out of the land, and the only way it can come out of the land is by work. The result that follows is, that the first element in creating an export trade is to place the labour that is useless at home on the land that is useless in other parts of the empire. We stand to-day in the condition when the balance between agriculture and manufacture has been disturbed, and when we can produce more manufactures than we can use and less food than we can eat; the effort must therefore now be made to re-establish the balance, by fostering a development of our agricultural power through a great emigration to our colonies.

The power of emigration as a means of developing our export trade can scarcely be overestimated; of what value are the exceeding poor to our manufacturers whilst they remain at home? What can be the consumption of English manufactured goods by that class, whose life is but one step above the savage? What can be the demand whilst care and want are the elements of life amongst a large portion of our English artisan class? And on the other hand, who shall place limits to their power of consumption when settled in other lands, where their every days toil not only produces for them the means to live, but the power of accumulating wealth to purchase whatever their inclination dictates? In this sense the growth of our population is a profound good for the manufacturing interest, if it be only properly utilized.

But looking at the subject from this point of view, the necessity for care and judgment in carrying the arrangement out in its entirety, becomes only the more apparent. It is quite true that our past emigration has fostered our export trade, both rapidly and decisively; but, that emigration was entirely different, both in class and character, from a free emigration carried out by Government aid; and the conditions that would evolve success and prosperity in the one case, might produce care and destitution in the other. We have therefore to consider what plan will be necessary to produce satisfactory results under the proposed conditions.

It is quite obvious that no arrangement can be made with the shifting bulk of poverty and semi-poverty to which the thought connected with Government aid naturally turns; it is equally impossible that any satisfactory arrangement could be made through the existing channels of emigration agency; the risk would be too great, and the difficulties too large. We must, therefore, turn to the assumption that satisfactory arrangements can be made through our various colonial governments. In order that such a supposition may not seem extravagant, let us remember what is proposed to be done, and what is the point aimed at. In the first place it is quite clear that no arrangement can be suggested to a colony that is not a direct benefit to itself, but it must at the same time be remembered that there is no benefit so direct and so unequivocally accepted as that of emigration, providing it be of the class required. We, therefore, start with the groundwork sound : the colonies want that which we are willing to give viz., population. The circumstances just now are peculiarly in favour of any arrangement being readily carried out; the best evidence of this is the desire, broadly and strongly expressed by the colonists themselves, for a more distinct and intimate union with England, beyond this, no condition would tend so absolutely to bind ourselves and our colonies together, as a great emigration carried out by arrangements between the colonies and the mother country. We have, therefore, two points clear: one is the desire of the colonies for our emigrants, and the other is the desire for a more intimate alliance with ourselves. It is not necessary to analyse the motives, or the conditions on which the last is based. It may be the desire, as has been very openly expressed, to have some portion of our army ready to do their fighting; or it may be the consciousness that the colonies gain in dignity by closer association; but, be it what it may, it answers all purposes, so long as the fact is so. We may, therefore, assume that with these feelings in existence, but little difficulty would be experienced in working through an arrangement with our colonies to receive, on equitable terms, our surplus population.

There are two distinct elements in the question of Emigration which it is necessary to clear up before we proceed further: the one is, the necessity that exists on our part to relieve ourselves of our surplus population, and the other is the advantage that our surplus population would be to our colonies. This last point has been considered so important by some of the writers in the public press, as to induce them to discuss the probability that the colonies would undertake the whole responsibility of the Emigration movement, and so relieve us from all further trouble. Putting on one side our own position and our own necessities, it is not by any means clear that our colonies would be at all disposed to take any such steps. It is quite true that our surplus population would be of enormous advantage to them, but it must be remembered that our colonies are growing rapidly by their own natural increase of population and by that portion of emigration which now exists, and although large emigration would be to them a great good and a great pecuniary advantage, it is not an absolute necessity. It must also be remembered that there is no special reason why the colonies should do now that which they have hitherto left undone. In the past, as well as in the present, it has always been in the power of the colonies to grant sums of money for free emigration if they had so chosen, but the advantages derivable by the colonies from such a course has never been sufficiently decisive to induce them to adopt it; and the temptations to such a step at the present time are naturally diminished in proportion as our necessities become more apparent. There are, also, important reasons on the other side why England should desire, and why it would be wise, that the mother-country should be the active agent in so important a matter. In the first place it will permit us the better to consult our own necessities, so far as excess of population is concerned; and, in the second place, it will the better enable us to discuss those tariff relations which ought to form so essential an element in any Government plan. The probabilities would therefore appear to be greatly in favour of the assumption that action must be taken by the Home Government if emigration is to be efficiently carried through; under such circumstances the question will again be as to how the money is to be employed, and how it is to be repaid. In order that the idea of Government emigration may be understood, it is suggested—

1st.—That emigration should, as a final resource, be absolutely free so far as immediate payment was concerned.

2nd.—That emigration should take place, as far as practicable, by families.

3rd.—That each emigrant should be entitled to a certain area of land for the purposes of cultivation, subject to Government control until the emigration money be repaid.

4th.—That each emigrant should bind himself to repay, to our own or the Colonial Government, the money advanced for his transit, as well as any expense incidental to his arrival in the colonies.

5th.—That such bond should be a first charge upon the land assigned to the emigrant.

6th.—That all money so advanced should bear interest at the rate of 3 per cent. per annum.

7th.—That all intending emigrants should be chosen by fitness, character, &c., &c., and those who could deposit a portion of their passage money to have the preference.

Assuming that the funds are forthcoming from the Imperial Government, as a loan at 3 per cent., to the Colonial Government, it may be asked, What is required from the Colonial Government? The answer is, that they shall make arrangements to find the emigrants work. Such an undertaking would entail considerable care and forethought, but ought not to present grave difficulty. In an old country where all the conditions and all the more marked requirements of life are already perfect, the difficulty of finding work fer new hands is always very large, but all the points that tell against an old country tell in favour of a new one. In England, for example, all our great public works are finished, in Canada and Australia most of the great public works have yet to be carried out; the land has to be cleared and tilled, roads to be made, houses to be built, and all the conditions of life that are complete at home have still to be perfected in our colonies, so that a vast field of labour lies open before them. But it must not be ignored that to prevent the labour from being too dense at any one place supervision and foresight is an absolute and unconditional necessity. So long as emigration is left to itself, the numbers of emigrants hold themselves in check, by the difficulties inseparable from emigration itself, and by the uncertainties that surround it; but, so soon as emigration becomes exceedingly easy, the numbers who will leave our shores will be so great as to necessitate some previous organization at the point of their destination, in order to avoid famine, disease, and want. This portion of duty should belong of right to the Colonial Government.

Assuming that the Colonial Government would be willing to undertake the responsibility, and, still further, to guarantee the interest and repayment of the money advanced, because of the obvious advantages connected with a large emigration movement directed towards their own shores, it may fairly be asked how can the Colonial Government see its way to secure the repayment of its own money? The answer is, that the labour that goes into the land is inalienable security. The land that is valueless whilst it was untilled, springs into value the moment the labour is placed on it, and we thus, by the mere action of labour, create value and security at the same time. This would be true with regard to all our colonies, but it has often been asserted, with reference to Canada, that there exists a constant tendency on the part of all emigrants, when they reach that country, to find greater temptations in the United States, and gradually re-emigrate there. It is, therefore, assumed as a probability that some such difficulty would belong to any large system of emigration to that colony: it may be answered, that no great undertaking can be carried on, involving the varying feelings and interest that belong to a great mass of people, without some such condition being possible. But the probability becomes exceedingly limited if the emigration takes place by families instead of by individuals. There is the unwritten law of life which binds men to their homes and their families, and those who would hesitate to desert their children in England, would exhibit the same hesitation in Canada; the bonds of feeling are strong enough to hold men under temptations far greater than this.

If, in addition to this, it becomes clear to the colonist

that by his own labour he can win for himself his own home, his own land, and his own independence, all probabilities are in favour of his abiding by his agreement. It has been demonstrated again and again that there is no spur so strong as the spur of property, and when a man sees before him the possibility and the probability of realising an absolute independence by his own labour, the temptation to remain where he is becomes overpoweringly great, and under these circumstances and with these prospects before him the labour that he will put on his ground is alike unstinted and unwavering. It will also be quite obvious that, when a colonist is settled on his land, he is bound by every tie to remain where he is, because the fruits of his labour are in it; and as the land improves under his efforts, it also improves by that which is not his effort, viz., the mere increase of population; and thus his capacity to repay the money lent him will grow and his chances of independence will grow in the same proportion. We have, therefore, two securities for the repayment of the money: the one is the man's own individual exertion on the land, and the other is the increased value of the property by the increase of population. Looking, therefore, at the whole case, there does not appear any grave difficulty in carrying out an arrangement that would be an aid to the colonies, advantageous to the colonist, and a benefit to ourselves.

It may be asked, Why should we so specially select our own colonies? If emigration is to be brought into action, why should we not make use of that plan which is at once the cheapest and most direct,—viz., a free passage to the United States. The answers to this are manifold. In the first place it is exceedingly dubious whether the United States would submit to a permanent continuance of a mass emigration from any country such as is here referred to. The facts connected with New York, and the other great seaboard cities of America, already point to the existence of a large mass of pauperism, doubtless due to the continuous influx of emigrants. So long as this is the mere action of private will and private enterprise, so long must the United States submit to a state of things which is a temporary evil, but which it cannot alter; but the moment the question passes from that of private action into that of Government arrangement, they would have a distinct right to protest, and no doubt such a result would follow so soon as our emigration was found to be more than the ordinary conditions of life in America could readily absorb. It has also been urged that by our aiding the emigration to America, we are in reality building up a great rival. It seems altogether beneath the dignity of our country to express any fear for the growth of the power of the United States, her greatness be it what it may, is in one sense a greatness of our own ; they are our descendants, shoots from a great parent stem; they inherit our language, our literature, and our laws, and they illustrate and enforce the value of those qualities on which we most pride ourselves; but, in the present state of their commercial relations, they have deemed it wise to enforce a tariff on all imported goods, that acts almost as a prohibition of our manufactures. In this course of policy, success is its own justification ; but, placed as England is to-day with an enormous manufacturing power that requires work, with a large population dependent upon its activity, it becomes a first necessity that any state aid that is given to emigration, should be given where the direct and indirect influences are the most decisively in favor of our home manufactures, and these conditions are best fulfilled by aid to our colonies.

The very magnitude and power of our colonial empire to aid us in our demand for increased commerce and to fulfil all that is required, become more distinct the more closely it is examined. The following facts will illustrate this :—

"Our colonial empire covers about a third of the earth's surface, and contains nearly a fourth of mankind. Its area is more than thirty times as extensive, and its population is more than five times as numerous, as those of the United Kingdom. It is estimated in the latest accessible official returns (in which, however, considerable discrepancies are noticeable) that its area is somewhat under 4,750,000 of square miles, and its population is somewhat over 155,000,000 of persons. Of this vast dominion about 1,000,000 square miles are in India, more than 2,500,000 square miles are in Australia, and more than 600,000 square miles are in North America. The population of British India is nearly 145,000,000, of British North America nearly 4,500,000, and of Australasia nearly 1,700,000. Our possessions in the West Indies (including Tropical America), the Cape (including Kaffraria), and Ceylon, have together an aggregate area of about 460,000 square miles, and an aggregate population of about 3,730,000 persons."— *Westminster Review*, Jan. 1870.

With a territory as large as that here depicted, embracing every condition of life and every variety of climate, there exists no obstacle to the development of a commerce immensely great. Not only this, but our colonies contain all the elements for the building up of a great outlying empire, fostered by the mother country, but controlled by themselves. Under these circumstances, the broad question is, in what relation ought we to stand to our colonies, and in what relation ought our colonies to stand to us? It would be mere waste of time to discuss the supposition that any set of circumstances would warrant us in endeavouring to guide our colonies by any more intimate imperial machinery than that which at present exists; whatever may be its value or whatever may be its failings, colonial representative government is an existing fact, and it would be impossible, even if it were wise, either to modify or change it. The whole course of events, not only throughout our colonies but throughout the whole world, points to a freer political thought and freer political action, and any policy that seeks to be permanent must contain within itself the germ of those conditions that will satisfy the needs of the future.

There is a mode of viewing our colonial empire which has originated with the idea that it is more trouble than it is worth, and if a country's policy were to be guided by irritability of temper instead of calm common sense, it would be quite possible to conceive conditions which would apologise for such opinions; but, as events are rapidly developing, the recognition that the enormous power our colonial empire possesses can be readily utilized, both in a monetary and social point of view, we may anticipate a very great change in our existing policy. Viewed in a large sense, our colonial empire may be considered as simply the outlying portions of Great Britain, which for the sake of convenience and economy now govern themselves, and which it would be at once our policy and wisdom to associate intimately with ourselves in our future career.

It may be difficult to predict the future, but it requires but little foresight to perceive, that our colonial empire must grow both rapidly and continuously. The mere mass of emigration that would flow from our shores would be a cause sufficient for such a result. The question is, how shall it be moulded? Shall it take the impress from our thoughts at home, or shall it grow into whatever form chance dictates? Shall we strive to make our colonies an integral part of the empire, and from which the future affords no reason to anticipate a separation, or shall we regard an eventual separation as the natural development of the life of a colony? The answer to these questions will depend upon the mode in which the whole subject is viewed. By those who regard war as the beginning and end of life, and peace a mere armed neutrality, by them our colonies will be considered sources of weakness and danger. But those who look upon war as a system fast dying out, and who see in the future an ever increasing necessity and an ever increasing probability of the permanent maintenance of peace—they will believe that the colonies contain within themselves the true germs of our future strength, ever developing silently the grandeur of our empire; whilst in the present they can absorb and use that surplus population which now festers in our streets and that surplus capital which is now lying by, waiting for employment. Under such possibilities the relation that we bear to our colonies and that our colonies bear to us becomes of grave importance. If wisely ordered, the whole relationship would become more intimate and more reciprocal year by year, and the little jealousies that now crop up would die out under the spell of mutual benefits, and we should grow together as the units of a great and wide spreading people.

We have now before us the rough outline of what emigration can be made to do. It can be made to release our overloaded labour market, reduce pauperism, and to help those who cannot help themselves. It can be made to act with enormous power upon the advancement of our commerce, and it can be made to build up with great force the undeveloped powers of our vast empire. All these things are more than possible, they flow naturally from our existing conditions. The question is, shall the effort be made? Shall emigration be organised and developed on a systematic plan, or shall it be left to drift as ciscumstances may dictate? Shall it be worked out by private aid, or shall it be a matter of state policy? The answer to these questions is not difficult to foresee: sooner or later the magnitude of the whole subject and the evidence by which it is supported, will force themselves so overwhelmingly on men's minds, that state aid in some form will be accepted as an unequivocal necessity. By an instinctive sagacity the working-men themselves feel that emigration is the true panacea for the existing condition of things, for, to use their expressive phraseology, "they are too thick here." It is curious, but none the less true, that the great underlying thoughts that guide national policy often commence at the base of society; the reason for this is not far to seek : the pressure of necessity forces on men the habit of continuous thought in connection with subjects which are essential to their own well being, and with limited knowledge, limited opportunity, and limited education, they thus seize with an intense force the point that is vital to themselves. It is thus that their opinion has value, it is thus also that they enunciate the necessity for free emigration, for they know their own need, and we may, therefore, be content to accept the plain common sense and practical thought that points out the permanent value of State aided emigration. Let us now consider the great question of our Indian Empire, and the means by which we can elevate the status of its people and promote the growth of our own manufactures.

CHAPTER VIII.

INDIA.

FROM what point of view are we to regard our great Indian Empire? Shall we be content to chronicle the brilliant deeds of Clive, Hastings and Wellesley? Shall we track out that line of policy by which a company of quiet merchants built up the grandeur of our Indian rule, or shall we turn to the every day conditions of life, and ask: What benefit do we, as a people, derive from that empire, which has been won by the genius, valour and toil of our great men? The tinsel of governing far reaching dependencies has shrunk into its natural proportions, and we have now reached the point where we no longer claim to measure our strength by the extent of our dominions, whilst it is long since that lacs of rupees formed the reward of successful pillage or atrocious mendacity. The very term—lacs of rupees—awakens in our memories the Begum speech of Sheridan, and the vigorous denunciations of Burke. It recalls from the pages of Macaulay those dramatic paintings of Indian society drawn from the life, whilst his words re-create into being the timid form of the crouching Bengalee; yet it is by comparing that past with our present, that we are enabled to recognise how fast our scope of thought has changed both in intensity and character. Within a few years our great dependency has passed from the rule of a company of merchants to be welded into the inner life of our empire, and that change recalls the question, of what use is India to us? We are no longer in the dreamland of poetry and imagery, but living in the midst of a pre-eminently practical age, and we, therefore, again ask of what use is India to us? Glorious as are the brilliant scintillations of genius that sparkle over the pathway of history, they are yet mere playthings when the struggle of life deepens in its stern intensity, and when through the mutterings of sorrow there rises the ever recurring question, how are the people to find bread? It is from this point of view that the great value of our Indian Empire can be best estimated, and from this point of view let us see wither it leads.

The conditions of the climate of India forbid our regarding it as the normal home of any portion of our race; on the hill-side, up the mountain fastnesses and in the Himalayas there may be parts that are suitable to our people, but as a broad whole India belongs to the dark skinned races. But India, with its area of 947,292 square miles and its population of 135,000,000 of people, possesses a capacity for the absorption of our manufactures so enormously great, whilst the result achieved is so infinitely little, that the circumstance challanges our attention. At the present time the total of our export trade to India is a little over 20 millions per annum, this amount ranking with our exports to America or the Hanse Towns. It seems an extravagant thing to say, but there appears no tangible reason why our exports to India should not be equal to our present commerce with the whole of the world; and if they do not become so it will be our own fault. A statement so broad as this requires some facts to justify it, and some explanation of the grounds on which it is founded. Let us place side by side two points, illustrative of the variations in our exports, and note the teaching. Previously to the outbreak of the Indian Mutiny our exports to India amounted to £11,666,714, in the same year our exports to Australia amounted £11,632,524; or in other words, the exports to India and Australia were about equal, whilst the population in India was one hundred times greater than that of Australia, the approximate number in both cases being: India, 135,000,000, and Australia, 1,350,000. If, therefore, we can so stimulate commerce in India that each individual could take from us one quarter the amount that each individual in Australia now takes, the result would be achieved.

Since the date of the comparison here instituted India has passed under Imperial rule; a larger force of Europeans has been stationed in the Indian Empire, railways have been built, and generally more activity infused into Indian life, our exports have doubled themselves and we have, therefore, so far started on the path of working the problem out, but even at the present the amount is so utterly disproportioned both to its area and population, that we are naturally driven to seek the reason why.

The reasons are not difficult to find, they are expressed in the two great causes—imperfect cultivation and imperfect communication. It is quite clear that, when a people is pressed by want and subject to famines, when its means for cultivating the land are utterly undeveloped, their power of purchasing our manufactures must be reduced to the very lowest ebb. It is equally clear that so long as the country has imperfect roads, no large improvement can take place, for each part will remain more or less isolated and the conditions of trade will be feeble and uncertain.

No error is more usual than that which associates with India the idea of enormous wealth. The traditions of our early conquests and the memory of our early successes have tended to foster this belief. The barbaric splendour of her princes, the hoarded lacs of rupees and the wonderful precious stones have all tended to distort our view and cause us to consider great wealth as the natural condition of life in India. It is only when men of the world place their experience plainly before us, and when the warnings of famine, like that which occurred in Orissa, stand clearly out, that we begin to recognise that India is very poor, but, she is poor, whilst she possesses wondrous capacities and contains within herself the elements of a boundless prosperity. In Mr. Chapman's *India* is the following:—

"The several topics of the poverty of the people, famines,
"and the land-tax may be grouped together, from their
"actual or supposed connection with each other. That the
"bulk of the population of India is extremely poor is, I
"believe, a fact no longer concealed from us by the present
"or traditional splendour of its princes, or by the ruinous
"magnitude of the armies it formerly maintained. The
"consequences of this poverty, and the means of remedying
"it, require discussions which do not permit space for inquiry
"into its remote history; but I may go so far as to express
"an opinion that it is by no means recently that India has
"fallen under this heavy disadvantage.

"Food, very scanty clothing, and often worse habitations,
"constitute at present the chief possessions of the majority of
"the Indian growers of cotton: a few hoarded rupees or
"jewels, and the means of making family shows, are the
"utmost of their hopes."

The implements of labor and the general ideas of the people are in perfect harmony with this description, and a few words place before us with almost photographic distinctness this element of life in our Indian Empire.

"But in Western and Central India there are almost no
"machines for raising water; certainly none moved by
"inanimate power. The wheel and pots, actuated by feet
"and hands of a man, and the direct pull of bullocks, in rais-
"ing a leathern bucket from a well, seem to be all the devices
"in general use. As to the employment of wind or water for
"any such purpose, it seems never to have entered the

"imagination of any of the natives; and a pump is altogether "unknown in the interior except to a few as a curiosity."

But if this be true as to the ordinary habits of life, still more instructive are the conditions connected with great tracts of country which to-day retain their original character in all their savage wildness. In some cases, one half of the area is cultivated, in others one third, and in some cases one thirtieth, these simple facts go to aid the explanation why we export so little to our Indian Empire.

In the north-west provinces the total area assessed was 49,150,995 acres, of which 24,177,161 were under cultivation during 1867—68. In the Punjaub the area is 106,768 square miles, of which 32,432 are returned as cultivated, 32,780 as culturable, and 39,556 as unculturable. The greater portion of that mentioned as culturable is situated in tracts where the rainfall is so scanty, that cultivation without irrigation would be impossible. The central provinces are thus described:— The south-eastern portion of the Nagpore Province is a great wilderness: that to the north of the Indrawatty is entirely uncultivated and uninhabited. The lower portion is described as a primeval forest; and, out of 114,718 square miles, which is the area of the province, 24,950 alone were cultivated. With regard to British Burmah it is said:—"The total area of this province has been estimated "at 90,070 square miles, of which one-thirtieth part is under "cultivation." These extracts, taken from our Government returns, will exhibit clearly the general characteristics of large portions of our Indian Empire; but the conclusion derivable from it becomes all the more absolute when the general state of cultivation and the general condition of the life of the people rise fairly before us. If the absolute area under cultivation is thus limited, we can understand how forcibly these conditions will tell upon our export trade, but still more will this be so when we recognise that the portion which is cultivated is rendered of comparatively little value, from the want of those sources of irrigation which are so absolutely necessary in a climate like India. All authorities are agreed that irrigation is the first necessity for successful cultivation, and all authorities are equally agreed that the means for carrying it out do not exist.

In some returns issued by the India Office, in July, 1869, entitled *Statistical Information with Reference to India*, are these remarks :—" One of the most important branches of the "administration of British India is that which is entrusted "with the development of the resources of the country by "means of public works. In a country like India the direct "aid of Government to industry is required for a variety of "purposes which in more advanced countries are sufficiently "and even better provided for by private enterprise. The "most important of these works are irrigation, by means of "which the land is rendered more fertile, and a certain "remedy is provided against the loss of crops during seasons "of drought, and communications which benefit not only the "staple produce of the country by providing means for its "export from the place of its production, but they also in a "like manner benefit the imports of the country, thus in-"directly stimulating the trade of other countries also."

In speaking of one portion of public works, and having reference to one product of India, a writer of considerable eminence adds :—

"If we look to any one measure of improved cultivation "as more important in India, and yet of more difficult "attainment than any other, we shall probably select irriga-"tion. Nearly every experiment tends to show that, in "some way or other, not yet much understood, the due "supply of moisture, whether to the soil or the air, neither "too much nor too little, nor at improper times, is an "indispensable element in the means of a successful growth

"of cotton. The natural advantages of the countries of suit-
"able temperature, both in India and elsewhere, which most
"cheaply produce cotton of acceptable qualities, seem to lie
"in a considerable degree in the fact, that their soil and
"climate fulfil, of themselves, this necessary condition in
"respect of moisture."

But what is so specially true of cotton is true of all other kinds of vegetation. The various famines that from time to time decimate India are due to the fact that irrigation works do not exist to supply the deficiency occasioned by long continued drought. The same writer adds:—

"But in the cotton-growing countries of Central and
"Peninsular India, irrigation, to be practised in the months
"when it is most needed, must be effected by cheaply and
"readily lifting water from wells, or from the beds of rivers,
"from 30 to 100 feet below the surface to be irrigated; a
"process of no great difficulty or expense, if suitable mechani-
"cal means were employed, especially where, as in many
"places, steady wind is mostly available. But there is no
"suitable skill in the country,—a deprivation the impoverish-
"ing consequences of which may be judged of when it is
"stated that irrigated lands, even in the districts near the
"Ghauts, pay three times as much tax, appear to afford ten
"or twelve times as much labour, and to yield twelve or
"fifteen times as much profit, as the same area without
"irrigation."

"The Concan is well known to grow little or no cotton;
"but it does not clearly appear whether this is owing to
"natural disadvantages or to other causes. The remarkable
"success of Mr. Elphinston at Rutnageree, is said to prove
"that nothing can be done in that quarter without artificial
"irrigation. . .. . . But Mr. Elphinston, at Rut-
"nageree, by careful crossing produced cotton of remarkable
"excellence, while, by irrigation, which cost nearly half of

"the first year's total expense of cultivation, he obtained "plants which eventually yielded a profit."—*Chapman.*

All this information points one way, that agriculture is imperfectly carried out and that irrigation works are a profound necessity. How, then, has the Indian Government dealt with a question which they themselves recognise as of paramount importance, both commercially and socially. The details of the amount expended are here given :—

Statement of Sums allotted for Irrigation Works during the past Six Years including State Outlay on Guaranteed and aided Irrigation Works.

1864—65	-	-	-	£510,322
1865—66	-	-	-	522,405
1866—67	-	-	-	645,482
1867—68	-	-	-	966,100
1868—69	-	-	-	1,205,100
1869—70	-	-	-	1,777,397

If it were intended to turn the whole subject into ridicule, nothing could be better fitted than these figures, and the proportion they bear to other portions of Public Works in India are worth noting. The following quotations are from the *Moral and Material Progress of India,* Printed by Order of the House of Commons.

" *Public Works.*—The expenditure on account of public "works in the Lower Provinces exceeded a million pounds "sterling, being considerably larger than in the preceding "year. It may thus be classified :—

By the regular Public Works establishments	£801,856
By civil officers in purchase of land for East India Irrigation and Canal Company in Cuttack - - - - -	11,582
By local establishments organized like the regular establishments - - -	103,003
And by civil officers - - -	90,652
Total -	£1,007,093

"The aggregate expenditure in the province of Oude on account of public works during 1867-68 amounted to £237,753, of which £27,435 was on account of establishment. £93,800 were expended on civil works, and £116,517 for military purposes. Among the former the largest items appeared under the heads of public buildings and communications such as roads and bridges. And under military expenditure that for barracks amounted to £90,871. A commencement was made last year towards the introduction of irrigation works into this province, for which object a staff of engineers had been appointed to survey the country and prepare a project for canals from the Sarda river."

Speaking of British Burmah :—

"The total sum expended in the province during 1867-68 on Imperial works was £248,538. The cost of the establishment connected with the above expenditure being £34,952. The sum expended from local funds, including cost of establishment, was £52,420. The gross income received in cash in the Public Works Department was £5,742.

"There are no public works for irrigation purposes in this province, but a large area of land has been reclaimed from swamp by the erection of a bund in the Myan-Oung district. Communication is kept up between the Rangoon river and the Sittang by deepening a stream which connects the Sittang and Pegu rivers, and is called the Pyne-kune creek or canal."

These illustrations will suffice to exhibit the position which irrigation holds in the midst of other public works, and from the facts and figures now given some judgment can be formed how little effort is made to meet this profoundly important requirement.

In rough words, the expenditure on works of irrigation may be considered as one million and a half per annum; how utterly inefficient such an amount is for carrying out the changes required over such an area as the peninsular of India, in its present condition, will be obvious to all who look at the facts for themselves. What value can flow to us, in a commercial point of view, from an expenditure so small that it is utterly inappreciable when spread over a great empire? At our present rate of action, five hundred years hence India may be properly irrigated, and our countrymen (if they are then traders), receive the benefit of the operation; but as regards our present or our immediate future, the whole thing is so trivial that its effects are utterly inappreciable. Yet the importance and need of more vigorous efforts are recognised by the Indian Office itself, but the difficulty of carrying out what is necessary arises from the whole condition of Indian finance. At the present time it requires all the care of clever men to establish a balance between income and expenditure, and this difficulty will be a permanent one so long as our great public works have to be paid for out of income.

There is great necessity for us to recognise how absolutely the poverty of the people re-acts upon, and limits, its trading capacity. No matter what the causes may be, so long as a people remains poor so long will it be unable to purchase largely of any manufactures. The first condition that stands before us in our endeavours to develope the commerce of India is that we must make India herself prosperous, for the first essential of all trading is the means to pay for what is bought, and this can only be done, in the present condition of life in India, by large works of irrigation spread throughout the country. The ordinary reply that will be made to this is, that all such undertakings are best left to private enterprise, and such an answer would be true in connection with ordinary trading transactions, but, under the special circumstances which surround our Indian Empire, the ordinary commercial system would not effect the purpose required.

Some illustrations are here appended connected with private enterprise.

"In the year 1859, a guarantee of interest on their capital "was given to a company formed for the purpose of con"structing works of irrigation in the Madras Presidency; "and in the following year a company was started to carry "out works of a similar character in the Bengal Presidency; "without the aid of such assistance from Government, but "the latter company having failed to raise the necessary "capital for carrying out their works, have, since the com"mencement of the present year, relinquished all their rights "in those undertakings to the Indian Government in return "for a repayment of the sums expended by them, together "with a small additional amount as compensation to their "officers, &c.

"With reference to the operations of the East India Irri"gation and Canal Company in Cuttack, a loan of £120,000 "was made to the company at the beginning of the year, to "enable it to prosecute certain works which it was unable to "carry out from want of funds."—*Progress of India*, 1869.

These two illustrations show, how, under the most advantageous circumstances, private enterprise is unable to carry through with success the works of irrigation that are known to be required; and this occurs not on account of the works themselves being unprofitable, but, because shareholders are unwilling to embark in enterprises which are so far removed from themselves and their ordinary habits of thought.

It is obvious, that enterprises of this kind would come into existence, only when the probable profits would be sufficiently large to cover all risks. But it is difficult to conceive that it would be the sound policy of any Government, to permit an organization which would be vital to the well being of its people to pass from its own control to that of others whose only motive could be the obtaining good interest for their money. Beyond this it is quite obvious, that such arrangements would lack the essential elements which underlie the idea itself. There are many parts of India, where irrigation works would be a lucrative investment; but there are other parts, where the results would be uncertain, and where also the true value would come indirectly; that is, more from the increase of trade than by large dividends from the works themselves. The result would, therefore, be that certain portions of India would be irrigated by Joint Stock Companies whilst the more remote parts would be left in their present condition. There are also other objections to such a system; it would be fragmentary, uncertain, and slow in its operations. Under these circumstances, the point desired to be achieved would utterly fail, for the condition of our home manufactures requires, that an effort should be made to develope our trade in connection with India, both rapidly and decisively. For this there are no means so certain as enabling the people to lift themselves out of their present poverty by the aid of irrigation works and good public roads. It will also follow that, by so aiding them, we shall aid ourselves, for their demand for our manufactures would increase in proportion to their means of paying for them.

Mr. Chapman, after giving some facts, adds:—

"From this instance it may be safely inferred that the
"readiness with which the natives of India, and even the
"lowest of them, fall into the use of manufactures, can
"hardly be exceeded in America; and the facts further show
"that *the use of our articles depends on our bringing into
"action the means of paying for them*, by affording employ-
"ment to the waste energies of the country and people. It
"should also be noted that the natives of India in general
"are so much more advanced than the Goands here spoken
"of, that their appreciation of the comforts and conveniences

"of life is much more easily awakened, and might clearly be
made to operate much more effectually in the establishment
and extension of commerce."

The necessity for large works of irrigation has now been briefly stated, but irrigation, powerful and important as it may be, is only one of the powers necessary to enable us to develope the commercial prosperity of India. The condition of the roads is one of equally vital importance and there are some points connected with their present state which are almost past belief. The special correspondent of the *Times*, writes as follows:—

"Bengal, under the jurisdiction of a Lieutenant Governor, is of the size of France and Switzerland combined, and how many miles of metalled road do you think it has? Not 500, or to be more accurate 498. I mean in the rural districts. . . . . There is no Parish system in Bengal. There is no link between the district officer and the thousands of villages under him. Hence, if anything is to be done, Government must do it; if the people have no stocks of food as in Orissa, half-a-million may die before the Government can know it."—*Times*, Dec. 6th, 1869.

"The roads in the interior are mere tracks; and even with important lines is this the case. In this matter the Deccan is probably not at all peculiar among native states."—*Moral and Material Progress of India.*

"In estimating the effect of want of roads on our exports, it must be remembered that the disadvantage commonly applies not so much to the cost of conveying our manufactures inwards, as to that of bringing to the coast the heavy agricultural and other produce which is to pay for them; and we shall see a few instances, both in America and India, where the effect is mitigated by the substitution of a lighter material of commerce. Notwithstanding, however, the occurrence of a few such instances, it must still be true, in

"general, that no country little advanced in the mechanical
"arts can pay for manufactures in other than crude and
"heavy produce; and such a country can make little progress
"besides that which is permitted by the means it may possess
"of cheaply transporting that produce to more advanced
"countries and more thickly-peopled seats of consumption.
"This, which is true of all countries, is especially so of India:
"the subject matters of its export commerce, if that com-
"merce is to be much extended, must necessarily, for a long
"time to come, be of a coarse and ponderous character; and
"by so much does its need of roads, and the effects of its want
"of them, afford a just parallel with the case of South
"America; the apparent exceptions also to the operation of the
"principle in both cases confirm its general truth."—*Chapman.*

The advantages here pointed out are curiously upheld by some remarks having reference to Mysore. The following is an illustration—"£14,722 was expended during the "past year, entirely upon village and district roads, with "the exception of small sums for wells and trees connected "with them; much good work has been done both in the "past and previous years, and the direct benefit of these "cross roads was reported to be of great value to all classes "of the community, but particularly to landowners."—
—*Moral and Material Progress of India.*

" By affording easier and cheaper means of transport, and
" by consequently enabling industrial products to be sent
" to more distant markets, railways undoubtedly not only
" enable home-producers to obtain higher prices from foreign
" customers, but also give a new stimulus to home-produc-
" tion, causing fresh lands to be brought under cultivation,
" or to be planted or sown with more remunerative crops,
" and encouraging equally the extension of manufacturing
" mining, and miscellaneous industry. Two distinct incre-
" ments of national wealth are in consequence made, consist-

"ing, first, of enhanced receipts from abroad for part of the "previous aggregate of national produce; second, of the "entire net profits on the sale."—*Chapman.*

The importance of good roads is unequivocally clear, for no large trade, either import or export, can be carried on where they do not exist. Hitherto the considerations have been directed to the influence that roads and irrigation have upon the general productions of India and the reflex action upon our export trade. But there is one more view which deserves to be considered in the possible value that India may be to ourselves and that is the relation it bears to our cotton manufactures by the growth of cheap cotton. At the outbreak of the cotton famine, the cotton that India supplied to our market immediately rose in value, and attention was also directed to the question whether it would be possible to grow better qualities. A number of experiments was made, and generally the result desired was achieved; but, even at the present time, the power of India may be considered substantially undeveloped. The following extracts will enforce this view. Mr. Chapman, after discussing an area fitted for the cotton plant, adds:—

"If one-half of it is occupied by mountain ranges, "sites of towns, beds of rivers, and unsuitable soils, the "other half contains 67,500 square miles, or 43,200,000 acres, "applicable to the growth of cotton fit for English use. If "one-fourth of this were cropped every year, and the produce "were equal to the average of Guzerat and Candeish, or "100 lbs. per acre, the weight of the whole crop would "be 1,080,000,000 lbs. per annum, or $2\frac{1}{4}$ times the entire "quantity annually consumed by the manufactures of Great "Britain, on the average of the thirteen years ending in "1846. But Indian cotton, of the quality at present supplied, "is not suited to more than 75 per cent. of our manufactures,

"that is, we could take from India only 360,000,000 lbs.
" per annum out of the 480,000,000 lbs. we now work up;
" so that this part of India alone, being probably capable of
" producing 1,080,000,000 lbs. per annum, could grow for us
" three times as much as we could take, and could therefore
" amply and fully stock us, even if we had no other source of
" supply, except for the very fine varieties required by a
" small part of our manufactures."

A writer in the *Cotton Supply Reporter* (Mr. J. Login, C.F., F.R.S.E.) also adds:—

" That of Egypt appears to me far in advance of anything
" I have seen in India, for, taking cotton as an example, one
" acre of properly irrigated land can produce eight or ten
" times as much cotton as the same area now produces in
" Northern India; so that, without increasing the area under
" cotton cultivation, I believe, by the introduction of the
" Egyptian system of agriculture into India, the produce may
" be doubled or quadrupled, without it being necessary to re-
" duce the quantity of land required for food. I have no doubt
" at all that cotton in much larger quantities, and of a better
" quality, could be produced in India by an improved system
" of agriculture. What I would venture to suggest is, that
" a dozen or two of Egyptian cultivators should be selected
" and sent to the various provinces of India, to aid in bring-
" ing about an improved system of farming, as possibly the
" natives may be more willing to listen to their advice than
" to that of Europeans."

It would, therefore, appear that the capacity that India possesses for producing raw cotton is practically unlimited. As we can consume enormous quantities of this article of her produce, India, in return, can consume enormous quantities of our manufactured goods. The conditions by which such a result can be achieved are still in the future; because those necessary elements, irrigation and good roads, do not exist. So long as these conditions remain unfulfilled, so long will it be that India will hold the inferior position with regard to ourselves which she holds at the present time.

All the points now referred to require, for their fulfilment, Government aid; private enterprise, even at its best, is inefficient and uncertain, and would deal only with minor points and on no general plan. Whilst the power that Government possesses to carry through any system is coequal with its own organization. In an article on India, having reference to the idea that the large public works should be carried out by government *The Westminster Review* has the following:—

"Every one is familiar with the usual stock objections
"to Government interposition wherever it can be dispensed
"with. That the state should do nothing for the public
"which the public can do equally well for themselves, has
"almost passed into a proverb, and far be it from us to
"dispute the soundness of the maxim. On the contrary,
"we are ourselves inclined to carry the proposition to an
"extreme. To us the fostering of habits of self-help and
"self-dependance, appears such an important element in
"national education, that within certain, and those pretty
"wide limits, we should say, better for the public to do
"things badly for themselves than to have them well done
"by others. But in saying this it is essential, especially
"where the construction of public works is in question, to
"distinguish carefully between the integral public and its
"individual components, as well as between countries in
"which the land belongs to individuals, and those in which
"—as in India, for example—the Government is the supreme
"landlord. Better, no doubt, that the inhabitants of a town
"or district in England, where the general principle of land-
"tenure is what it is, should make their own roads, docks,

" bridges, gas-works, and water-works, than pay for having
" them made by the Central Government; but if the local
" community will not itself undertake their construction, it
" by no means follows that the next best thing is to leave
" them to be constructed as a commercial speculation by
" private adventurers. For with respect to public works, it
" is desirable, not only that they should be as suitable as
" possible for their special purposes, but that the public
" should have the use of them on the cheapest possible con-
" ditions, which they obviously cannot have if private specu-
" lators are permitted to make profit by them; while without
" the prospect of profit speculators will not undertake them.
" That surely cannot be the best arrangement for the public
" under which public needs become the subject of private
" gain, under which individuals profit at the expense of the
" general. Evidently it were better, if possible, that what-
" ever gain is made at the public expense should go back
" into the public purse.

" So soon as the doctrine that the land belongs to the
" people as a whole shall obtain complete recognition, road and
" canal making, and irrigation on that gigantic scale which is
" essential to eastern countries, will be found to be among
" the few important functions of Government, when restricted
" to the proper sphere of its activity.

" The more attention is given to the question—Who
" ought to construct the public works?—the more distinct
" we believe will be the answer that the duty rests with the
" Government. Assuming that political economists and
" statesmen will ultimately concur in this judgment, they
" will probably be also of opinion that whenever such works
" would undoubtedly yield a large indirect profit to the state,
" by developing and enriching it as a whole, they ought to
" be constructed even though they should fail to yield a
" direct profit on their cost and management."

There are some points connected with India about which there can be very little doubt. There is no difference of opinion that so long as a country remains imperfectly cultivated, devastated by famine, and without roads, it must of necessity be poor. These are the conditions of India to-day, and they can only be removed by changing the circumstances that have produced them. If the first essential of successful cultivation in India be large irrigation works, as all competent authorities concur in asserting, it is quite clear that, so long as these do not exist, imperfect cultivation must be the rule. But if irrigation works were erected throughout the entire of the Indian Empire, the question would only be half answered: roads and railroads are equally as imperative necessities, if India is to be utilized to us as a great market for our manufactures. No large advance in India can take place without improved cultivation, and no large trade without improved roads: the one is a complement of the other; they are each good, but to be fruitful to us in a commercial point of view, they must be combined. A step has already been taken with reference to the construction of railroads, but to what extent and on what scale may be judged by the fact, that we have spent five times as much money on railroads in England as we have engaged to spend on the railway system of India.

The policy that governs a country must vary from time to time and change as circumstances change. It may have been that the policy which guided the old East India Company was true and sound for their time and their circumstances, and they therefore could afford to reap their harvest from a less anxious policy than what is needed now. Placed as England is to-day, it has become of very high importance that every power we possess, whether acquired by military daring or built up by commercial prudence, should be utilized for the good of the people at home. Our colonies need no such consideration; but we are placed where the struggle of life deepens with an ever increasing intensity, and where the need for work has made such a policy of ever increasing importance. It is from this point of view that India can largely aid us, for she can be made to absorb year by year a larger amount of our manufactured goods. But there is one point pre-eminently clear : we can only aid ourselves by first aiding India; we can only create markets for our goods by first creating the conditions by which they can be paid for; and we can only create these conditions by a large expenditure of public money on public work. The probability that such expenditure will realize good interest is borne out by the results which appear in connection with our Indian railways. And the probabilities are still larger in connection with those works that are the more immediate agents in the production of national wealth.

The conditions here pointed out all lead to one conclusion : the necessity on the part of Government to undertake this responsibility. But the construction of vast public works will require an entire change in the existing financial policy of India. At the present time there appears a distinct objection on the part of the Imperial Government to any loan being contracted by the Indian Government. It appears to be held that the various improvements that are required shall take place by private enterprise or be paid for out of income; and the consequence is that India must languish for want of that money which now lies waste at home.

The present condition of our money market affords a curious commentary upon this position. Lord Overstone, in a late debate in the House of Lords, stated that the absolute nett growth of capital was about 150 millions annually; and sooner or later the question will arise, what is to be done with it ? It is easy to find speculative adventures and unsound investments; it is easy to lend to defaulting governments and repudiating states, but it is not so easy to find legitimate openings for investment, that will yield a moderately large percentage and at the same time be absolutely safe. It is not difficult to see that in England we have already a plethora of capital, and that the tendency is for that plethora to increase. In the first place, money has now been for some years at a very low rate of interest, and the great bulk, that has been taken from our market, has been taken in foreign loans. In the next place, it is equally clear that in 1866 the capital of the country was more than equal to all its emergencies, and nearly four years have gone by since then. If we then take Lord Overstone's estimate as being right, we have had an accumulation of capital of more than 500 millions since the panic, and under existing conditions this accumulation is still going on.

It must also be recognised that so long as our export trade continues at its present amount, the profit produced by it will be nearly as large now as on any past occasion. The same may be said with reference to the existing incomes of those who hold realised property. The depression that now exists will fall, as it has fallen, on the artisan, the shopkeeper, and the manufacturer; whilst the surplus incomes of the wealthy will remain intact. We shall, therefore, have a profit always accumulating and nearly as large, at the present time, as it would be under more favourable circumstances; the difference being that in prosperous times all classes benefit, whilst, under existing circumstances, only a limited number, but that limited number is represented by the class of capitalists.

It should also be remembered that the demand for money at home in the future will be relatively small. The capital necessary for building our railways, making our docks, erecting our warehouses, constructing our machinery, and generally perfecting the conditions of our working and social life, already exist and any demand in the future in connection therewith must be limited. We are in the position of a merchant with a workshop attached to his house; we have built and furnished our house, erected and fitted our workshop, and constructed, in every way, the arrangements necessary for our business and our living, and the money that was required to put us in this position, when once expended, does not require to be expended again; very little thought will show that such is substantially our case. In the first place, since the introduction of our railway system, we have spent over 480 millions of money in perfecting it; but, once being finished, it will not require rebuilding. The same may be said of our docks, warehouses, manufactories, dwelling-houses, &c. It is of course quite true that a certain amount will be spent annually in keeping the arrangements of our country in their proper working order, but beyond this it would appear probable we shall not have at home much employment in the future for our savings. So that in the ordinary course of events, with the accumulation of capital continuously going on, we shall have a continually increasing mass of deposits, which will seek employment and will have great difficulty in finding it. If these illustrations be correct, we have capital seeking outlets and India requiring capital. The question, therefore, rises up:—Shall these two conditions be made mutually beneficial to each other? Shall we elevate our Indian Empire by the aid of English capital expended upon large public works of commercial utility, carried out under Government inspection and built by the aid of Government loans; and by so doing help to renovate into fresh life our now stationary export trade?

RESUMÉ.

At the outset of this book the question was asked, How are the people to find work and food? and this question is forced upwards from the condition in which England stands to-day. We have an enormous pauper population, and a population still greater just above pauperism. We have an export trade that is stationary; a limitation in the demand for labour through the introduction of machinery; a decrease of employment through the force of foreign competition, and, to intensify all these, we have a population whose increase is at least six hundred per day. How are these conditions to be dealt with? It is idle and weak to speak of the great wealth of England as a panacea for our present evils, whilst starvation exists in our streets and pauperism and destitution threaten to overwhelm us. The weight of our present position is beginning to produce its natural effect, and men, who are usually removed from the impulses that guide public life, are looking around them and saying, where is this to end? It is known that manufacturers are wasting the fortunes, which they had amassed in the past, in the endeavour to keep on their mills at half-time. It is known that every kind and every class of employment are not only filled to overflowing, but the applicants are hopeless in their endeavours to obtain work. In the streets of London, men are to be found by thousands who are ready to toil and cannot find the work to do, and, as week passes week, fresh circumstances continually crop up, showing that underneath all this, there are states of destitution still more terrible; and it is thus, that the question comes fairly home, how is this to end? If the subject be played with; if men fold their arms and look on; if they say, as has been said before, that all this will right itself, then the law of self preservation will be powerful enough to sweep away the existing organization and place us face to face with difficulties more profound and more real than any that this country has ever had to contend with. The difficulties of our position become all the more clear the more closely they are viewed, and instead of being linked with any individual or passing influence, the causes are general and the results are general also.

In the earlier chapters of this book, the subject has been briefly and rapidly traced out, with the facts on which it rests and the evidence by which it is supported. What is the broad teaching that it contains? what are the causes of our present position? and what is the conclusion to which it points? Plainly and clearly and past all questioning stands the rough fact that we cannot feed ourselves; equally clearly, and equally definitely, stands up the second fact that the numbers we cannot feed are ever largely on the increase. These two truths represent the great elements of the whole problem; but the teachings they contain and the consequences to which they lead are either not recognised, or recognised with the lazy indifference with which we regard unimportant facts. Yet they underlie our whole commercial policy, will mould the conditions of our future, and are vitally important, because the conditions that belong to them will grow with an ever-increasing force. No man doubts the broad fact that we cannot feed ourselves. It has been accepted by Parliamentary Committees, made the plea for large Inclosure Acts, and it caused the repeal of the Corn Laws; equally as little can it be doubted that this condition is ever on the increase, for it is shown by the Registrar-General's returns, and the ever increasing competition for work. Day by day the tell-tale of our population mounts higher, and its results are to be found in the increasing requirements for foreign food. But at great Manchester meetings men tabulate out this enormous increase, and appeal to it as an evidence of the value of free trade; whilst the facts are that our imports of food have only the one meaning, viz: we import that food which we cannot produce for ourselves. The relation that food thus bears to our population makes itself felt in a variety of ways: it changes the character of our pauperism, the conditions of our destitution, and the price of food itself; it also enforces the importance of our export trade and the danger of foreign competition. All these circumstances, so apparently remote, are linked together by the one tie, that our land cannot feed our people.

With respect to the first point, the state of our pauperism, it is so changed that it no longer represents its original elements. The first poor law was based on the idea that paupers were the idle and the worthless, and to such a labour test was the natural limitation of help; but to-day men seek work and cannot find it, enforced idleness saps energy, and thus it is they sink slowly down to pauperism. The same may be said of destitution with even greater force: that silent, hopeless, broken misery, which is too powerless to create work, too feeble to force it, and too proud to beg— that poverty which sinks, suffers, and dies; that destitution, of all others the most fearful and the most real, also springs from over population.

This influence of over population also manifests itself in the ever advancing price of food: silently and steadily, various kinds of produce are ever on the increase, and this increase makes itself felt through various channels. It can be traced through trade-union strikes, and the power of foreign competition. When men struck for higher wages, they made use of a plea at once vigorous and sound; they stated that they required more wages, because the money would not purchase so much now as it would have purchased some years ago, and it is thus that the claim for higher wages has a moral basis and a political meaning. This advance in the price of food becomes even more important, when we trace the relation it bears to that struggle of continental competition on which we are now entering. It is true that England draws her corn from the granaries of the world, and it is equally true that we reap an advantage by so doing, for we have no longer the enormous fluctuations in value to which corn was previously subjected. But when those countries from which we draw our corn are also entering into the race of manufactures with ourselves, it is clear that they start with this condition of life in their favour, for they only sell to us their surplus food. We must therefore recognise that some portion of their power of competition, depends upon circumstances which we are powerless to change. All men will agree that throughout the Continent the means of living are cheaper than they are with us; if we add to this, better climatic conditions, greater abundance of food and less density of population, we have the explanation why wages are lower on the Continent, and why, even under equal conditions of life, Belgian cottons and Prussian iron can be sold cheaper than our own. This continental competition which is now growing so rapidly, and which will grow still more rapidly in the future, is produced by the same influences as those that affect us at home—increase of population. The whole of Europe is becoming more densely peopled, and the density of population is awakening a fiercer struggle for life, and from this comes competition in our various manufacturing products. It is important for us to recognise that France, Belgium, Germany, and other countries can manufacture more cheaply than we can, and it is still more important that we should clearly recognise the reason why this is and the probability that exists of its increase.

It has been suggested, that the way to meet the difficulties incidental to foreign competition is to impose duties on foreign goods and to insist upon the principles of reciprocity, but any attempt to deal with this difficulty through the influence of protection would be idle and worthless. It is possible that heavy import duties would help that portion of labour which belongs to our home manufactures, but such duties would help labour at the cost of the whole nation. Beyond this the result would be altogether trivial when compared with the total manufactures of our country; and it is quite clear that, in the open markets of the world, protection could have no existence. Our struggle for life is not limited to the area of the British Isles, for our commerce stretches over the whole globe and has to compete in all markets. And the warnings, that now rise from the pressure round our very firesides, will tell us how the force of the same competition will be, sooner or later, co-equal with our commerce. Let us then carefully consider the whole question. Let us recognise, that we are in the midst of a dilemna which springs from a surplus population, ever on the increase, and pressing every day more severely on the means of life. Let us also recognise that this difficulty is still further intensified by the existence of a foreign competition, that is not only large in the present, but promises to increase with still greater force in the future. And let us recognise still further that this element of foreign competition grows not only by the pressure of population in France, Belgium, and Germany, and by the advantages of food, position and climate, but also by those accumulations of capital that are now to be found on every large exchange in Europe.

How then are we to meet these difficulties, and which way is our position drifting? To answer these questions we must recognise where we have been and where we now are. A century ago it would have been possible for us to have shut ourselves up in our island home, and lived utterly excluded from the outside world. The land then yielded sufficient produce to feed the then existing population. To-day the case is so utterly changed that we are dependent upon other parts of the world for one-half of our food: the difference between these two conditions marks the change between the past and the present. In the past we were dependent upon the yield of our own soil alone for the food that we ate, and our export trade was simply the exchange of superfluities. To-day, our numbers are more than the land can feed, and we are therefore dependent upon the amount of our export trade to pay for the extra food we require. Unless our export trade grows with the growth of our population, we shall have the destitution, misery and death that we have in our land to-day ever increasing.

There are men who so utterly misunderstand this relation, that they point to this expansion of our export trade as though it were the embodiment of all success, and they see in its enormous growth a theme on which their fancy can dilate. But when it is reduced to the hard realism of life, the growth of our export trade simply means, that there have been so many more people to work and so much more work has been done. It will therefore follow that the continuous increase of our export trade is as much a matter of necessity as the increase of our importations of food are necessary to feed our ever increasing people. We may be gratified when our export trade expands, because its expansion indicates that the people have employment, and we may be equally warned when it ceases to expand, for then the people will starve. The conditions of the question will, therefore, resolve themselves thus: in the past we fed ourselves entirely from our own land; in the present we feed ourselves partly from the land and partly by the aid of our export trade. What are the probabilities that surround our future, and how can the necessary balance be maintained in the face of a rapidly growing population?

The answer to this question is, that we can keep the balance either by the continuous expansion of our export trade or by reducing the number of our people by the aid of emigration. But to arrive clearly at our conclusions, we must ascertain by what means our trade has grown in the past, and which of these causes can be depended upon for its growth in the future? Also, what is the condition of our colonies at the present time

Let any man turn to the map in this book and note how our export trade has grown: at times it remains stationary for years and then springs forward, it once more becomes stationary, then again advances. What is the explanation of such phenomena? It is to be found in the action of special causes. For instance—it cannot be doubted that the discovery of gold in California and Australia developed our export trade, and equally as little can it be doubted that the introduction of the railway system brought people into more intimate relations and developed commerce. Beyond these, the effect of wars and exhibitions is to bring people into more intimate relations, and so to lay the foundation for increased trade. That wars exercise such influence upon trade is a matter of reasoning, but the teachings derivable from our exports to France, Turkey, Russia, India and China, in connection with our military operations, all seem to point to the conclusion that the reflex action of war is to increase trade. Our exhibitions were also constructed on the thought that, by bringing together the various nations of the world to exhibit their special productions, we should increase trade, and the results that followed appear to uphold it. New markets and speculative manias have also aided this result. But the question here arises, how many of the same influences can we reckon upon for our future trade? Exhibitions have ceased to be novel; Gold Discoveries no longer create their first enthusiasm; the Railway System in Europe has produced its first great changes, and the revolution of thought and life it introduced will grow slowly in the future. War happily is becoming every day more deprecated, and every day less probable. New markets come but rarely, and the results of our speculative manias have caused men to dread rather than respect them. All these causes—causes which were powerful in our past for the rapid growth of our export trade—afford us but little hope for the future, and there appears no reason to anticipate that we shall be able to awaken analogous powers to supply their places without making distinct efforts for ourselves.

There are some who so misconceive the whole question as to assert with strange pertinacity, that the entire of the increase of our past trade has been due to the action of free trade, but the facts do not warrant this. All men are more or less agreed in the general truth of Free Trade doctrines; and placed as England is to-day, free trade is her soundest policy; but the endeavour to build up the whole of the wonderfully complex relations of trade by one simple idea, is as futile as it is unreal. If free trade were the all powerful element that its too enthusiastic advocates would make it, how comes it that trade ever slackens? How comes it that America, with an excessively high tariff, continues to import ever increasing quantities of foreign manufactures? The answer, as a matter of free trade reasoning, is difficult to find, but as a matter of every day common sense it is clearly on the surface. Our trade grew during the last twenty years because new stimulants were applied from time to time, and it has ceased to grow because no new stimulant is forthcoming. Let any man look at the figures from 1848 and see how the trade grew;

not gradually, but by bounds; and note also, when it thus rebounded, some definite and known causes are clearly responsible for the result. Let any man again look at the totals of our export trade from 1815 to the present time and he will then see that until 1848 it never definitely grew. It varied from year to year, but its changes were changes only; our exports in 1815, 1840 and 1848 are substantially the same. It would take too long to trace out the conditions of the earlier times referred to, but it may be broadly stated, they are removed from the question of protection duties. With regard to high tariffs in America they act there as they act everywhere else, they check consumption and they check it to the extent that the price of the goods is increased by the duty. This influence is lessened when a population is rapidly increasing both in numbers and prosperity, as is the case in America to-day, and under the special circumstances in which that country is placed the question of import duties has a different significance from what it has with ourselves. With us, any modifications that we can make in our import duties, so as to stimulate foreign trade will be the best course open to us. If our home territory were large enough to feed our population, our dependence on foreign countries would cease, and the question of the importance of our foreign trade would be reduced to the very smallest dimensions. But such a condition not being possible, we are driven to consider by what means we can increase our future trade.

It is important for us to remember, that the necessity that our trade shall grow with increased force in the future is proved by conditions not at first sight on the surface. Not only is it true that foreign competition is growing with great rapidity; not only is machinery lessening the demand for labour; but the construction of our great public works which has hitherto afforded employment to a large number of our labouring classes, may be considered as completed, and this source of employment will, therefore, exist no longer. The combination of these causes render more imperative the necessity that new channels for our commerce and new arrangements for dealing with our surplus population should be brought into action. What those arrangements could become will be more apparent when we trace out the possibilities and powers of our Colonial Empire.

Our Colonial Empire, exclusive of India, has been reckoned as one-quarter of the world, and now contains a population of about ten millions. It is found, that this colonial population absorbs, at the present time, a large and continually increasing quantity of our exports, and that any large accession to their numbers, by way of emigration, causes a direct increase in the amount. The facts connected with our export trade to Australia and California arising from the emigration to these countries, may be considered conclusive proofs of such results; and it would therefore appear, that any course of action, which will develope emigration, will also develope our export trade. It may, therefore, be said, that the first element out of which to build up an increasing commerce exists within ourselves, for we can stimulate emigration as we will. It is found that this increase in our exports is always greater in connection with emigration to our colonies than with that to America or elsewhere. It would, therefore, appear that it will be to our advantage that the current of our emigration should be directed to the finest portions of our Colonial Empire. The value of emigration, both to the colonies and ourselves, is accepted as an established truth, and the desire is generally expressed for its increase. But as to the manner in which it shall be carried into effect there is large divergency of opinion. On the one side there are those who insist that, in the existing conditions of society, emigration should be carried out by means of State aid; whilst, on the other side, there are those who insist that the ordinary influences of life are equal to all emergencies, and it would therefore be unwise to interfere in any way. The question is, which of these is right? The advocates of State aid reply to the doctrine of our allowing things to work themselves out, that such a course would be productive of profound misery, and they point to the past conditions connected with Ireland as an illustration of the truth of their opinions; and when under such circumstances the people died by hundreds of thousands. Such a course may have been palliated by the teachings of political economy, but it was not statesmanship. If this result were true of Ireland twenty-four years ago the truth is equally pregnant with warning for our own land to-day, since we have in the midst of us a population of one million of paupers and another population of two or three millions of people but one step above pauperism, whilst the trade by which they are fed is stagnant and waning. Leave these conditions alone, let the problem work itself out, give no help: and what must follow—starvation or revolution. The one is the dictum of political economy, the other has an uglier name.

It would be undesirable, that any such results should come to pass whilst the means to avoid them are at our command, and these means are at our command in the proper use of our Colonial Empire. In it we have the elements out of which can be woven a great social and a great political triumph. On the one side we have land lying useless, myriads of acres waiting to be tilled. At home, we have an enormous surplus population, crushed by sorrow and want, lying hid in dingy courts and close alleys, and ever generating and dispensing the elements of physical and social disease. So long as they remain with us, so long will these conditions intensify, until at last, by the mere magnitude of the danger, we shall be driven to face the question whether we will or no. Let us at the same time recognise that these very elements, so prolific with evil,—evil alike for themselves and others, are the very elements out of which good can be woven. The circumstances by which such a result can be achieved are plainly before us. Let us bridge over the ocean that lies between ourselves and our colonies; let us place the labour that is useless here on the land that is useless there, and the danger that now menaces us, and the sorrow and want that now surround us would cease of themselves. To effect this result thoroughly and efficiently, Government aid is required; for Government alone has either power or knowledge sufficient to deal with so great a subject. The plea that individual energy, private benevolence, or parish organisation should be left to work the result out is a mere evasion of the difficulty, and not a solution of it, for even at their best they would fail. Individual energy is crushed out in those cases where men are steeped in poverty and utterly broken down; private funds already slacken and, at their greatest strength, are utterly inadequate to the magnitude of the necessity; and parish organisation has neither knowledge of nor association with, our colonies sufficiently large, to enable them to deal with the question as a whole. Government, on the contrary, has all these points, and so soon as it gets over the mental difficulty, and recognises that it is at once its wisdom and duty to undertake it, all other difficulties will disappear. It is not necessary to discuss the various suggestions that are supposed to be involved in the idea of Government aid. The vital question is, is such a step necessary? The answer to this is to be found in the one fact that we have an annual increase of population of more than two hundred thousand persons for whom no work exists at the present time, and for which there is no probability of work in England in the future; this one condition affords the explanation of the need for Government aid.

The objections, that have been raised, spring from views of the relation between Government and people that belong essentially to the past; the traditional ideas remain, even when the spirit is dead, and it is thus we have disinclination or apathy, even when no clear reason can be given. But as we have now arrived at a period when a Government may be supposed to represent the necessities of a people, the probability is very large, that under the pressure of events, the mode in which this subject will be viewed will undergo a marked change. We shall have the question of Government aid to emigration first ignored, then discussed, and finally passing into the condition of an accepted necessity. Common-sense suggests its prudence and its value, for it is clearly wise, that the aid given to those, who cannot help themselves, should be such as will place them in a position where they will be enabled to earn their own living and where they can also indirectly aid our manufactures; and by no means can this be done so efficiently as by aid to emigration. There are also large reasons why this question should not be considered or treated as a local one. Our poor, concentrate where they may, are the poor of the nation; special circumstances may have driven them into special localities, but questions of parish arrangements lose their significance in the face of great national difficulties like those of the present, and we are thus entitled to ask that the question shall be dealt with as a whole, and not in detail. Under our present conditions such a course becomes at once a necessity and a policy: a necessity to remove from our shores that labour which vainly seeks for work; and a policy because emigration would not only relieve us from our surplus population, but would at the same time develope and increase our export trade.

The idea of Governmental interference has yet another arena, the condition of our Indian dependency calls loudly for its exercise. Without challenging either the wisdom or justice of the rule of the East India Company, there are yet some broad facts clear. For nearly a century a large portion of our existing territory has been under their rule, and yet India to-day is so undeveloped that her capacity to absorb our manufactures is at a very low ebb, and it is at this low ebb because the means for cultivation, such as works of irrigation, are imperfect; and the means for communication, such as good roads, are imperfect also. Their is no denial of the fact that India is very poor, and there is equally little denial of the cause from which that poverty springs. It is accepted on all sides that the imperfect condition of her agriculture, the paucity of irrigation works, and the absence of good roads, are the more immediate causes of the poverty of the people. It may be assumed that it is to us a wise policy to stimulate the wealth of the natives of India—altogether apart from any question of humanity or good government, because in stimulating the material well-being of the natives of India, we create the means by which our own manufactures can be purchased. The present condition of India is so remote from its possible capabilities that we can only speculate as to what it might have been under different circumstances. How far the East India Company is responsible for these defects, and how far it is our duty to see that they are removed, will depend upon the view that may be taken of the functions of government. If it be considered that our position in India is simply to rule, that is, to maintain our position and uphold our status as the conquerors, then roads are mere military necessities, and irrigation works are of very dubious advantage. But if our position is to govern India, and to govern her so that we can elevate her people by developing their material resourses, and aid ourselves by creating new markets for our manufactures; in such case, large expenditure by Government on internal improvements is a profound necessity. If these conditions be carried out, India, with her myriads of people, will grow rapidly in wealth, and the consequence will be, that her power to absorb our manufactures will grow rapidly also. With India thus growing, and with our Colonial Empire absorbing our surplus population and each year consuming larger quantities of our goods, the means by which we can solve our present difficulty appear fairly before us.

The condition of our country is fast changing, and we are on the eve of a new national life. Through much bloodshed and through many changes we have built up our position of to-day, and noble as it is, it is yet chequered with danger and full of warning. It is true, that our export trade has grown in the past with sufficient rapidity to meet our necessities, but there have been times, when, from the fact of its not so growing, enormous misery and wide spread destitution has been the result. Such was the state of our country from 1836 to 1846, those ten years spoke of bread riots, discontent and sedition, and we must not shut our eyes to the fact, that since then we have passed through strange and stirring episodes. Some twenty years ago the Bank of England was fortified, and London in the possession of the military; it was believed that the phantom of revolution that had swept over Continental life would be re-awakened in our own streets. The danger was imminent; for political discontent was surging through the land; chartist orators roused the people to a sense of their misery and the mutterings of revolution swept far and wide, and all this was so, because trade was slack and poverty was everywhere; these conditions are once more reappearing, and will once more produce the same results. It may be said that history chronicles our military triumphs, reproduces our state treaties and dwells upon our royal pageants; but its real life lies far lower, it is to be found in that silent growth of thought that moulds our institutions and builds up the fabric of human society, and it is thus that the well being of the people to-day becomes one of vital importance. Everywhere the conditions are unsound and unsatisfactory, poverty is stalking through the land, and hunger, that great teacher in the past, is also the great teacher in the present. The wild upheaving of the first French revolution, which changed the entire structure of European society had its origin in the same cause; the want of bread. The warnings long preceded the event, the passionate teachings of Rousseau and the bitter sarcasms of Voltaire were bandied from mouth to mouth, and spread throughout the land, because they appealed to existing sorrows, and the people who knew the depth of their own misery, clung with passionate intensity to that teaching, which promised a better future.

We too have had the teachings that were to regenerate society; and these panaceas appeared in Chartism, Socialism and Land Schemes ; how far these ideas were true, how far worked out, and how far opposed to the profoundest elements of human life does not now matter, they were taught and they were believed. That this could have been possible marked clearly the state of the people at that time—marked their sorrow and their poverty. That danger passed away through the influence of an accident. The discovery of gold in California and Australia and the consequent vivid awakening of our export trade found work for the people, and it was under such influences that the dogmas of political theorists and the dreams of philanthropists and philosophers sank to their natural level. Under such influences the thought of the people passed from the questions of revolution to the construction of trades' unions and building societies. Once more we have lived past our prosperity, and once more we stand in the position, where our trade is checked whilst life is rapidly on the increase, and where, through such adverse conditions, we are drifting back to the same point once more to re-awaken our old discussions. To-day the indications are everywhere around us, they may be found in the uneasiness of society, in the special discussions that now press forward in politics, in the broad and often repeated assertion, that the land is the heritage of the people, and that our national success is the success of the few and not the success of the many. All these signs are signs of warning, and it is well for us to note their meaning. We are all too apt to forget how slight is the structure of our past success, and how short is the time that separated us from great danger—our commercial greatness is limited by about twenty years—and immediately behind that time, arose the threat of revolution. It is true that we lived that difficulty down as we should have lived down a greater, but the teaching is none the less real. Since then we have had the vision of universal peace paraded before us and the assertion that England would grow to be the workshop of the world. That dream is already a dream of the past: war has made itself felt, other nations have entered the race, and although we are still the great traders of the world, the singularity of our position has gone. America, Germany, France, Switzerland and Belgium are all competing with us in every market, and it is therefore necessary for us to note the change of our circumstances and mould our position into accordance with them. It is true that in the open race we are no longer alone, but it is equally true that we have still enormous advantages over all other nations and these advantages only require utilizing to enable us once more to bound forward in our career, and to distance all competition. Those advantages are to be found in the value of our Indian dependency and in the enormous area of our Colonial Empire. Let us but aid India in accordance with her requirements; let us but weld together our colonies so as to form them into an integral part of our empire, let us but utilize that money which now lies idle in our markets, or seeks outlets in foreign loans; let us but aid emigration largely, freely and with well planned schemes, and the growth of our commercial prosperity will be greater than the most enthusiastic dreamer could picture. But these conditions require energy, decision and care, those great elements of English character, never more conspicuous than when most required.

THE END.

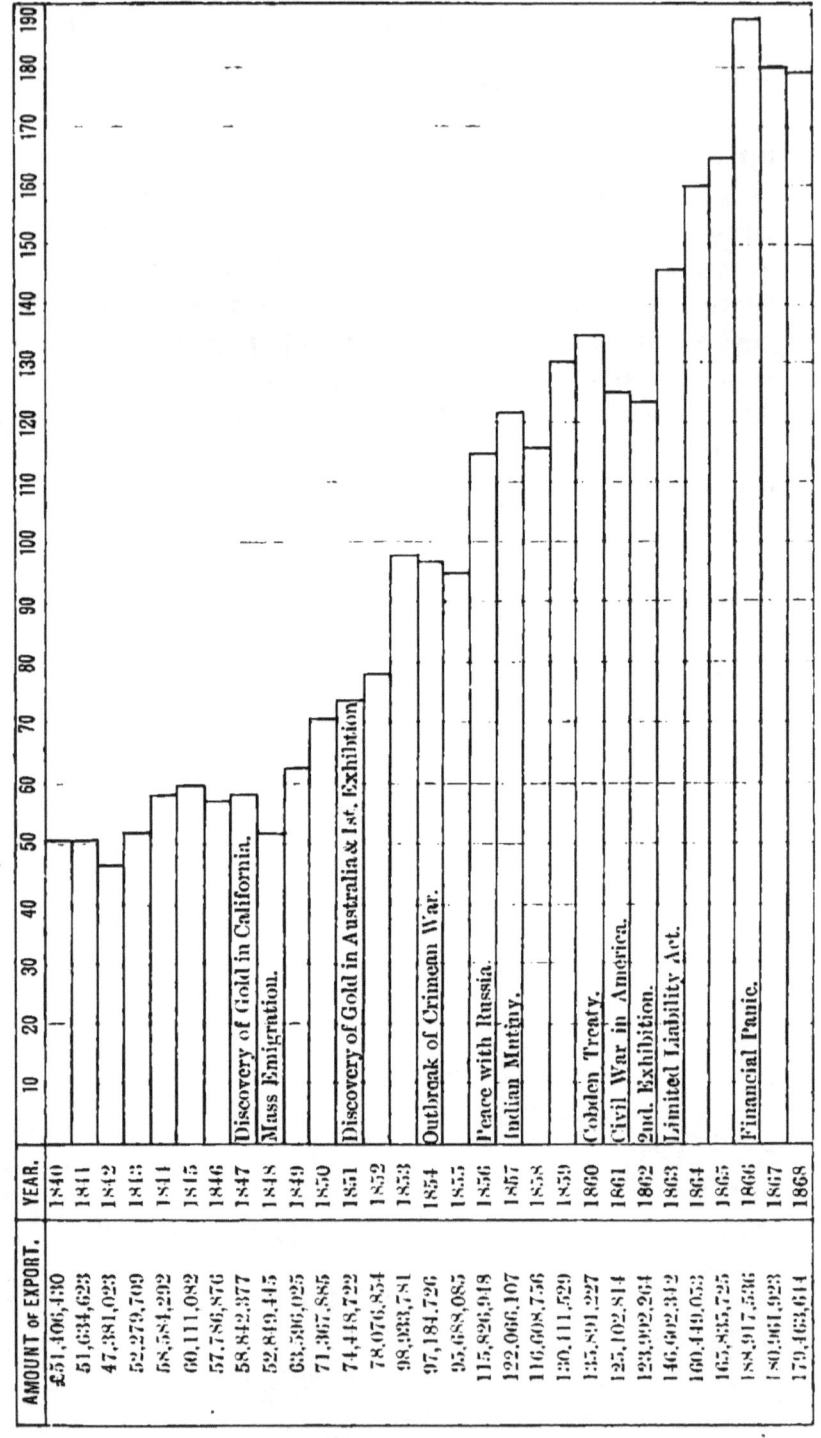

www.ingramcontent.com/pod-product-compliance
Lightning Source LLC
Chambersburg PA
CBHW020827190426
43197CB00037B/723